MW01701273

Clare -
Thanks for your
contributions to
education!
[illegible signature]

CONCEPT DEVELOPMENT

A Hilda Taba Teaching Strategy

May 2013

SHELAGH A. GALLAGHER, PH.D.

Royal Fireworks Press
Unionville, New York

Copyright ©2012, Royal Fireworks Publishing Co., Inc.
All rights reserved

Royal Fireworks Press
First Avenue, PO Box 399
Unionville, NY 10988-0399
(845) 726-4444
fax: (845) 726-3824
email: mail@rfwp.com
website: rfwp.com

ISBN: 978-0-89824-860-9

Printed and bound in the United States of America using vegetable-based inks on acid-free, recycled paper and environmentally friendly cover coatings by the Royal Fireworks Printing Co. of Unionville, New York.

TABLE OF CONTENTS

INTRODUCTION

The launch of Sputnik in 1957 spawned a generation of innovative works in education. Many focused their efforts on curriculum, resulting in such timeless pieces as *Man: A Course of Study* and the *Biological Science Curriculum Study*. Hilda Taba and her colleagues were a part of this curriculum zeitgeist. Working primarily in social studies, Taba published important practical and theoretical curriculum works. But she didn't stop there. Taba balanced her efforts in curriculum with a parallel emphasis on a refined description of inquiry-based instruction. The inductive instructional strategies she developed broadened the scope of her work so they apply across subject domains.

I was introduced to the Hilda Taba teaching strategies as an M.Ed. student at the University of Arizona. Dr. C. June Maker, who had studied at the Institute for Staff Development in Florida, required a course on the Taba strategies and developed her other methods courses using Taba's carefully structured question sequences and close, detailed self-assessment of pedagogy.

I wish I could say that I immediately recognized the Taba strategies as transformative teaching tools, but it's not true. At the time, I thought Taba and her colleagues had simply created a nit-picky, micro-managing approach to writing lessons. It wasn't until after I had graduated and used the strategies with both children and adults that I came to realize the paradigm-shifting nature of her system that uses thoughtfully planned question sequences and nuanced instruction to develop higher-order thinking.

More than 25 years later, my notebooks of Taba materials are still among my most prized professional possessions. To my mind, these materials should be integral to pre-service instruction, peer coaching groups, and professional development. They are of enormous value to anyone interested in refining their classroom practice.

This book draws from seminal pieces of Taba's repertoire, including the 1967 edition of *A Teacher's Handbook to Elementary Social Studies* and *A Teacher's Handbook to Elementary Social Studies: An Inductive Approach,* published posthumously through the efforts of Mary C. Durkin, Jack Fraenkel, and Anthony McNaughton. I also drew upon training materials prepared at the Institute for Staff Development and on Mary Durkin's 1993 book *Thinking through Class Discussion*.

Four appendices are included to provide additional detail on topics related to Concept Development. The first two, *Thinking throughout Concept Development* and *Types of Groups*, introduce additional layers of depth and complexity to the Concept Development lesson. The third is a transcript of a 1971 presentation by Mary Durkin, one of Taba's team of colleagues, in which she highlights important features of the strategy. The fourth appendix includes blank lesson plan forms and cognitive maps for your own personal use.

CHAPTER 1: THE HILDA TABA TEACHING STRATEGIES

One scarcely needs to emphasize the importance of critical thinking as a desirable ingredient in human beings in a democratic society. No matter what views people hold of the chief function of education, they at least agree that people need to learn to think. In a society in which changes come fast, individuals cannot rely on routinized behavior or tradition in making decisions....[T]here is a natural concern that individuals be capable of intelligent and independent thought. (Taba, 1962, p. 216)

TABA'S APPROACH: INDUCTIVE REASONING

Constructing a house requires beginning at the bottom and building up; starting with the roof doesn't work. Builders first pour a foundation and then add the frame, floors, and walls. Finally, with all the supports in place, a roof is built on top.

Hilda Taba approached teaching thinking in the same way: from the ground up—an inductive approach. Taba believed that, just like roofs, higher-order thinking is built upon a strong foundation—a foundation of quality information. Thinking skills combine with facts to build walls around the foundation. Finally, with foundation and walls in place, students can construct the highest-level ideas—abstract generalizations. Together, facts, thinking skills, and abstract ideas form a cohesive set.

Each of the Taba teaching strategies is designed to develop a different set of skills. While there is some discrepancy about how many strategies Taba developed, the materials created by the Institute for Staff Development include four: Concept Development, Interpretation of Data, Application of Generalization, and Resolution of Conflict. Several "secondary strategies" are also referenced in Taba's work, such as Concept Attainment.

These strategies are grounded in the theories of Tyler, Piaget, Vygotsky, and Ausubel. They also reflect Taba's assumptions about learning:

> *. . . [thinking] skills will arise from a dynamic interaction between the student and the stimulation he receives from well-phrased and carefully sequenced questions, from interesting and socially significant content, and from the kind of classroom climate which encourages free-ranging and uninhibited responses.* (Taba, Durkin, Fraenkel, & McNaughton, 1971, p. 65, emphasis added)

Several of Taba's assumptions about the nature of thinking and learning are encapsulated in the statement above.

THE FOUR TABA TEACHING STRATEGIES

Strategy	Purpose	Lesson Sequence	Skills Developed
Concept Development *Generalization* ↑ *Facts*	Derive abstract principles from concrete facts.	• List • Group and Label • Subsume • Regroup • Generalize	• Identify shared attributes • Categorize • Select appropriate terms • Develop hierarchies of ideas • Engage in flexible thinking • Create abstract generalizations
Interpretation of Data *Causes* ← *Facts* → *Effects*	Starting with a set of facts, predict direct and indirect consequences, and infer direct and indirect causes.	• List data • Determine direct effects • Infer indirect effects • Determine direct causes • Infer indirect causes • Create a generalization based on evidence and inferences discussed in the conversation	• Identify and list relevant data • Identify direct causes • Infer direct consequences • Identify/infer indirect causes and consequences of events • Draw direct connections between data and inferences • Create abstract generalizations
Application of Generalization *Generalization* ↓ ↓ ↓ ↓ ↓ *New Facts*	Test the fit of an abstract rule or principle by applying it to a new set of information.	• List what might happen using the principle in a generalization • Identify necessary conditions for listed events to occur • Infer possible consequences of listed events • Provide evidence to support inferences • Affirm or edit generalization (principle) based on conversation	• Apply general principles to specific circumstances • Use existing principles to predict future events • Use known principles to explain new information • Create causal links between facts and principles

Strategy	Purpose	Lesson Sequence	Skills Developed
Resolution of Conflict/ Exploring Feelings *Cognitive and Affective Understanding* *Problem*	Students explore a variety of dimensions—affective and cognitive—involved in solving different kinds of problems.	• Identify relevant information in a problem scenario • Infer possible actions and emotional responses of different people • Propose and defend possible solutions • Infer reactions to proposed solutions • Relate the situation to other, similar problems, and describe emotional responses • Identify criteria and evaluate solutions • Conclude how people deal with these situations in general	• Interpret feelings, values, and attitudes to solve a social or human relations problem • Explore feelings, values, and attitudes behind human behavior • Generate alternatives for action in a problem • Predict possible short- and long-term consequences of alternatives • Choose a justifiable alternative based on specific criteria

Thinking can be taught.

Underneath this assumption lies a secondary assumption that all students can improve in their ability to use higher-order thinking skills. Taba's research demonstrated that students of varying abilities can make improvements as a result of using her methods.

Students can reach higher levels of thinking using a small quantity of quality information.

Taba questioned the assumption that children need vast quantities of facts before they can learn higher-order thinking skills. She demonstrated through her strategies that students can develop higher-level thinking skills using relatively small quantities of relevant information.

Thought processes evolve in a "lawful," or natural, sequence.

Taba did not focus on individual thinking activities, but on complete thinking sequences that cultivate higher-order thinking. Many familiar thinking skills are embedded in each sequence; however, the strength of the Taba strategies is in the natural progression a lesson follows from initial facts to final abstract generalizations.

Higher-order thinking is achieved through structured question sequences.

Questions are the centerpiece of the Taba strategies. Open-ended, focusing questions form stepping stones that lift students from lower-order to higher-order thinking. Probing questions draw students into deeper levels of thinking within each stage. Consistent with the view that questions are vitally important, the strategies are supported by two tools to help cultivate students' questioning skills. The Cognitive Map helps teachers plan question sequences, and discussion analysis forms help teachers self-asses their classroom discussion technique.

Meaningful generalizations are formed by working with information in depth.

Higher-order thinking, according to Taba, is the result of a "dynamic interaction" between students and content—a continuous interaction that runs the course of a lesson. This approach ensures that students understand the direct connection between facts and generalizations. Generalizations created as the result of working in depth with information tend to be both substantial and complex, not "bumper sticker" tag lines at the end of a lesson.

SYSTEMIC, REFLECTIVE ATTENTION TO INSTRUCTION

The Taba strategies invite instructors to be deliberate in all aspects of instruction, from lesson planning to self-assessment. The system built around the lessons helps ensure their success and cultivates teacher skills in questioning and active listening. Elements of this instructional system include:

Advanced Planning. Taba's research demonstrated that preparing focusing questions and anticipating student responses in advance are important elements of a successful discussion. She developed the Cognitive Map to assist in the planning process.

Questioning. The Cognitive Map allows teachers to "see" how thinking will unfold in a lesson, allowing them to plan questions to propel the conversation from one step to the next. Taba's research on questioning practices revealed the significant influence seemingly innocuous questioning habits can have on a lesson. She developed a set of recommended practices to follow throughout an inquiry-based lesson, including habits that promote or discourage student participation. A brief introduction to these practices is presented in Appendix C.

Instructors who pay close attention to what students say will be able to respond with follow-up questions that probe or shift the discussion—a skill that empowers both teacher and student.

Reflective, Self-Aware Instruction. The third component of the instructional system is a set of materials that allows teachers to self-assess their skill in classroom discussion. Starting with a basic discussion analysis, the materials proceed to attend to very specific details that can affect student engagement and ease.

The structures built into the Taba strategies do not make them rigid, teacher-proof, or "dumbed down." Instead, the structure allows for more sophisticated instruction. Experienced teachers find flexibility in the topics they choose, in their selection of questions, and in the specific ideas they pursue in depth during a discussion.

A System of Support for Successful Instruction

Plan

Focusing Questions

and

Cognitive Map

Concept Development Step	*Focusing Questions*	*Materials and Supports*
Step 1: Listing Data	*What is an example of food that comes from nature?*	• Provide pictures of food around the room. • Refer students to textbook. • Allow students to talk to a partner for a minute before gathering list.
Step 2: Grouping and Labeling	*Grouping: Which items on our list can we group together based on an important shared characteristic? Why do these items go together?* or *Which items could go together because they are alike in an important way?* *Labeling: What 1-2 word label would best describe this group?*	• Provide guidelines: Students must create at least xxx groups and can have no more than yyy items left. • Give students time to Think-Pair-Share before beginning class discussion • Use 2nd Column to record answers • Change marker color • List groups then go back and label
Step 3: Subsuming	*Which of the items under one group could also go under another group?* *or* *I see that 'corn' is under the group Starch. Where else might 'corn' fit? What makes you think that 'corn' could belong in that group?*	• Change Marker colors • Show hierarchy by listing in outline form on the board
Step 4: Regrouping and Labeling	*So far, so good! Now what completely new ways can you find to group the items on our list?* *If necessary: If you shift your thinking away from food groups and towards other aspects of food, what new groups do you see?*	• Change marker colors • Provide time to think before discussion.
Step 5: Generalizing	*Based on our original list, the groups we've created and the way we subsumed the groups, what would you conclude about the food we get from nature?*	• Give students a minute of individual think time to write down ideas before discussing as a class. • Gather a few ideas and then select one to edit one or two as a class to incorporate other ideas

Cognitive Map for Concept Development

Purpose of Discussion: ____ *Extend and clarify the students' concept of human dependence on nature.*

Possible List (Step One)	Possible Groups and Label (Step Two)	Possible Subsuming (Step Three)
		Possible Regrouping Step Four)
Possible Generalization(s) (Step Five):		

Grouping and Labeling: Anticipate groups and labels students will create

Teach

List	*Groups and Labels*	*Subsuming*	*Regrouping*
1. Steak 2. Peaches 3. Apples 4. Pineapple 5. Pears 6. Ham 7. Green beans 8. Carrots 9. Celery 10. Rice 11. Wheat 12. Tomatoes 13. Salmon 14. Milk 15. Chicken 16. Cheese 17. Shrimp 18. Seaweed 19. Eggs 20. Yogurt 21. Potato 22. Honey 23. Beans 24. Oatmeal 25. Broccoli	**Sometimes Stored** Peaches Apples Pineapple Pears Green Beans **~~Meat~~ Protein** Steak Shrimp Ham Chicken Salmon **Starch** Rice Beans Potato Oatmeal Wheat **Vegetables** Carrots Celery Broccoli Seaweed Tomatoes Potato	**Sometimes Stored** *Tomatoes* *Ham* *Vegetables* **Starch** *Rice* *Wheat* *Oatmeal* *Beans* *Potato* **Complete Nutrition** *Starch* *Protein* *Vegetables*	**~~Ground Grown~~** **Farmed** Pineapples Carrots Celery Potato **Animal Produce** Cheese Eggs Honey Yogurt Milk **Water Based** Rice Salmon Shrimp Seaweed
Generalizations: Humans gather, grow and preserve food from nature. Nature creates a variety of food that man eats to stay healthy and alive.			

Reflect

Discussion Analysis

PRACTICE

Finding patterns in classroom interactions requires taping a 5-10 minute segment of a Concept Development lesson. It will help to start taping as a part of your standard practice so that everyone becomes accustomed and comfortable with the presence of the camera.

Record five minutes of your Concept Development lesson. Set the camera where it will get the best recording of teacher-talk. While student talk is important, the primary focus of this analysis is what you (the teacher) says.

Part 1: Classroom Interaction Analysis

Using the chart below and chart the path of your classroom conversation using the code.

T = Talk A = Ask M = Management

Teacher																						
Students																						

Teacher																						
Students																						

Teacher																						
Students																						

Teacher																						
Students																						

Count the number of times you enter each code for you (Teacher) and for your students. Include a subscript to distinguish between individual students, if desired. Put the totals in the blanks at the bottom of the page

Teacher	*Students*
Talk ______	Talk ______
Ask ______	Ask ______
Open	
Close	
	Manage______
	Number Participating______

Question Count	
Teacher	*Student*
Open	*Open*
Close	*Close*

CHAPTER 2: FROM FACTS TO GENERALIZATIONS IN FIVE STEPS

The ability to think cannot be "given" by teachers to students. Effective thinking depends on the richness of content, the processes used, and the initial assistance provided in the development of such processes. (Taba, Durkin, Fraenkel, & McNaughton, 1971, p. 11)

THE FIVE STEPS OF CONCEPT DEVELOPMENT

Concept Development is probably the easiest of the four Taba strategies. In fact, one might wonder why an entire book would be devoted to such a straightforward process. It's true that most teachers do a good job of learning Concept Development fairly quickly; it's equally true that those who take time to get to know this strategy find many opportunities to make small but meaningful refinements to their instruction.

A Concept Development lesson has five steps. Each of the five steps builds upon the one before, adding a new level of complexity. Together, the steps create a natural stairway from facts to generalization. The steps are listed below. The chart on the following page shows a completed Concept Development lesson on nature.

Step 1:	List	Gather a list of about 25 items that can be placed together under one category.
Step 2:	Group and Label	Group and label the items from Step 1.
Step 3:	Subsume	Cross-categorize items and/or create a hierarchy of ideas using the items and groups from Step 2.
Step 4:	Regroup	Set aside groups and labels from Step 2, and create completely new groups using the items from Step 1.
Step 5:	Generalize	Make broad but relevant statements about the nature of the items on the list based on insights gathered during Steps 1-4.

(Taba et al., 1971)

The fundamentals of teaching Concept Development are quite easy: the steps follow in a natural sequence, and students move automatically to increasingly complex thinking. At the same time, there is a great deal to explore beneath the surface of the strategy, with many opportunities to draw added value from the five simple steps. The example in this chapter walks through each step in detail, providing examples of some of the many teachable moments that can occur in a Concept Development lesson.

TIMING

A Concept Development lesson typically lasts around 70-75 minutes. The chart at the top of page 13 gives a general sense of how long each step takes for most fourth- through twelfth-grade classrooms. Students in grades K-3 will move through Concept Development more quickly because they work with fewer items. For these students, a Concept Development lesson lasts around 30-40 minutes. These are just approximate times, however. The actual time will vary depending on students' familiarity with the strategy and the intended goals of the lesson. Suggested ways to break up a lesson over two or more class periods are presented in Chapter 5.

PROGRESSION OF A CONCEPT DEVELOPMENT LESSON

Purpose of Discussion: *To extend and clarify students' understanding of interactions among elements of backyard nature*

Grade Level: *Elementary*

Source of Background Information: *Personal experience*

First Focusing Question: *What are examples of nature in your back yard?*

Step 1	Step 2	Step 3	Step 4
List	***Group and Label***	***Subsume***	***Regroup and Label***
Leaf Dogwood Tree Daffodil Grass Dirt Black Ants Worms Dew Dandelion Pine Tree Raccoon Deer Crabgrass Rain Butterfly Bush Honeysuckle Poison Ivy Oak Tree Maple Tree Rabbit Chipmunk Sunshine Moss Red Ants Snake	**Trees** Pine Oak Maple Dogwood **Plant Invaders** Poison Ivy Dandelion Honeysuckle Crabgrass **Grass-Related** Dew Regular Grass Sunshine Rain Moss **Forest Animals** Raccoon Chipmunk Deer Rabbit Snake **Bug Life** Dirt Red Ants Worms Black Ants	**Plant Life** *Trees* *Grass-Related* **Forest Animals** *Bug Life*	**Animal Food** Grass Butterfly Bush Rain Maple Tree **Garden Elements** Dirt Honeysuckle Daffodil **Familiar Animals** Chipmunk Rabbit Deer Black Ant **Garden Helpers** Worms Rain Sunshine

Step 5

Generalizations: *Nature provides food and a place to live for animals; nature takes care of itself. Even a small bit of nature has many different elements. Nature provides food and shelter for each creature.*

Step	*Time*
List	5 Minutes
Group and Label	20-25 Minutes
Subsume	10-15 Minutes
Regroup	20-25 Minutes
Generalize	15 Minutes

CLASSROOM PREPARATION

Concept Development is not a complicated strategy and does not require an elaborate set-up. Classroom preparation is fast and straightforward.

1. Use butcher paper, a whiteboard, or a smartboard separated into four sections to keep a record of the lesson, (low-tech butcher paper is often the most flexible option). Remember to leave space on the board to record students' generalizations at the end of the lesson.

2. Provide students with a copy of the organizer, or have them recreate it in their notebooks.

3. Gather four different colored markers, one for each column of the chart; this helps students keep track of the different steps.

4. If possible, select a student to write on the board so you can focus on the classroom conversation.

5. Have a copy of your Cognitive Map available for reference.

6. Review Appendix A and Appendix B.

BOARD LAYOUT FOR CONCEPT DEVELOPMENT

List	*Group and Label*	*Subsume*	*Regroup*
Generalizations:			

CONCEPT DEVELOPMENT LESSON PLAN

One of Taba's core beliefs was that "...[thinking] skills will arise from a dynamic interaction between the student and...well-phrased and carefully sequenced questions" (Taba et al, 1971, p. 65). If carefully sequenced questions are necessary to develop thinking skills, then anticipating question-and-response patterns becomes the centerpiece of lesson planning. Carefully planned questions are like a trailblazer's marks, carving a path through the material to the desired goal. The purpose of the Cognitive Map is to help teachers anticipate how students' thinking will develop as the lesson proceeds. The example below presents a Cognitive Map for a lesson on human dependence on food. Fifth-grade teacher Mr. Todd used the Cognitive Map to consider the list he'd like students to work with, the kind of groups they are likely to create during Grouping and Labeling, and so on. Having seen the lesson unfold in his mind's eye, he's ready to ask himself, "What question will get students to suggest these items for the list?" and "What question will encourage them to group in ways that show them something important?" These questions are the heart of his Concept Development lesson plan. The final Cognitive Map and lesson plan for Mr. Todd's lesson are presented on the following pages.

COGNITIVE MAP FOR A CONCEPT DEVELOPMENT LESSON

Purpose of Discussion: *To extend and clarify the students concept of human dependence on nature*

Possible List (Step 1)	*Possible Groups and Labels (Step 2)*		*Possible Subsuming (Step 3)*	
1. Apples 2. Steak 3. Peaches 4. Raisins 5. Pineapples 6. Pears 7. Ham 8. Green beans 9. Carrots 10. Celery 11. Rice 12. Corn 13. Tomatoes 14. Chicken 15. Sausage 16. Milk 17. Plums 18. Cheese 19. Shrimp 20. Peanuts 21. Eggs 22. Yogurt 23. Potatoes 24. Wheat 25. Oatmeal	Fruit Apples Peaches Pineapples Pears Raisins Plums Vegetables Green beans Carrots Celery Corn Tomatoes Starch Potatoes Rice Oatmeal Wheat Peanuts	~~Meats~~ From Animals Ham Chicken Sausage Steak Shrimp Eggs Dairy Cheese Milk Yogurt	Vegetables *Potatoes* Starch *Corn* ~~Meats~~ From Animals *Dairy*	
			Possible Regroups and Labels (Step 4)	
			Green Green beans Celery Pears Apples Grown Pineapples Potatoes Peanuts Corn Carrots	Breakfast Foods Yogurt Eggs Oatmeal Sausage Protein Chicken Cheese Peanuts Steak Ham

Generalizations (Step 5): Humans depend on nature for all food. Nature provides a way to create food.

SAMPLE FOCUSING QUESTIONS FOR CONCEPT DEVELOPMENT

Lesson Plan: *Concept Development*
Grade Level: *Elementary.*
Purpose of Discussion: *To extend and clarify students' understanding of a human dependence on nature*
Background Information for Lesson: *Personal experience*

Concept Development	*Focusing Questions*	*Materials and Supports*
Step 1: List	*What are examples of food that come from nature?*	• Provide pictures of food around the room. • Refer students to textbooks. • Allow students to talk to a partner for a minute before gathering the list.
Step 2: Group and Label Mr. Todd likes to include the word *important* because it deters grouping based on the first letter of the words or other trivial reasons.	Grouping: *Which items on our list can we group together based on an important shared characteristic? Why do these items go together?* or *Which items could go together because they are alike in an important way?* Labeling: *What one- to three-word label would best describe this group?*	• Provide guidelines: Students must create at least five groups and can have no more than five items left. • Give students time to think-pair-share before beginning class discussion. • Use second column to record answers. • Change marker color. • List groups; then go back and label.
Step 3: Subsume	*Which of the items under one group could also go under another group?* or *I see that "corn" is under the group "Starch." Where else might "corn" fit? What makes you think that "corn" could belong in that group?*	• Change marker colors. • Show hierarchy by listing in outline form on the board.
Step 4: Regroup	*So far, so good! Now what completely new ways can you find to group the items on our list?* *If necessary: If you shift your thinking away from food groups and toward other aspects of food, what new groups do you see?*	• Change marker colors. • Provide time to think before discussion.
Step 5: Generalize	*Based on our original list, the groups we've created, and the way we subsumed the groups, what would you conclude about the food we get from nature?*	• Give students a minute of individual think time to write down ideas before discussing as a class. • Gather a few ideas, and then select one or two as a class to incorporate into other ideas.

WHEN TO USE CONCEPT DEVELOPMENT

The skills developed in Concept Development are important and useful throughout the curriculum; however, the strategy is not designed for daily use. Concept Development is best used selectively to introduce, punctuate, or draw connections between ideas.

Introducing a topic:

Example: A first-grade teacher begins a lesson on communities by having students list, group and label, cross-categorize, and regroup members of a community. The generalizations students create at the end of the lesson are then used as touchstones throughout the unit. As students learn more about communities, they revise the generalizations, extending the ideas they created during the Concept Development lesson.

Reviewing a topic:

Example: A high school social studies teacher helps her students review for a test by having them use Concept Development with 25 factors that led to the Civil War. In the process of grouping, subsuming, and regrouping, students construct ways of organizing, and thus remembering, the information for their test. They also come up with some interesting ideas for essay answers!

Organizing information for reports, papers, and projects:

Example: A parent homeschooling her 12-year-old son shows him how to organize ideas for an essay using Concept Development on the topic of his choice. Outlining can be a bone-dry topic to teach, yet it's essential to high-quality secondary work. Concept Development provides an engaging way for children to discover how to create hierarchies of ideas for papers, PowerPoint presentations, or oral reports.

Understanding fundamental ideas and principles:

Example: A fifth-grade math teacher has her students bring in an example of a graph as a homework assignment. She then uses Concept Development to identify the elements of graphs and the relationship between those elements and the information they provide.

Drawing relationships:

Example: A middle school science teacher has had her students working in small groups, each investigating the features of different aquatic biomes. After they have gathered their information, each small group contributes five critical features of their biome to a list for a Concept Development lesson. The purpose of the lesson is for students to see similarities across the biomes, since the group research has focused primarily on differences.

What Is a Concept?

Trying to figure out what someone means by *concept* can be confusing; the word is used in many different ways. Sometimes *concept* refers to a broad, overarching idea like *truth* or *continuity* or *structure.* Other times *concept* is used to describe topic headings like *habitats* or *government* or *characters.* Taba used both forms of *concept* in her work, calling the broad, overarching concepts *Key Concepts.* Which kind did she intend to be the focus of Concept Development? She provides an explanation:

The concepts talked about here are the building blocks for...generalizations. In that form they are...to be distinguished from the Key Concepts,...largely because the concepts discussed in this strategy are part of a process which assists and usually precedes the development of generalizations. They are therefore less abstract and inclusive than Key Concepts which are highly abstract labels. (Taba et al., 1971, pp. 65-66)

What Is Generalization?

The word *generalization* can be just as confusing as the word *concept*; however, the American Heritage Dictionary does provide a succinct definition: *A principle, a statement, or an idea having general application.*

Like concepts, generalizations can be written at different levels of abstraction. Abstract, universal generalizations are considered one of the highest levels of reasoning. However, it is important to remember McNaughton's cautionary note:

...the most effective [generalizations] are those which have the greatest amount of depth...invested in them. Less effective are those which are so abstract that their meaning is vague.... (McNaughton, cited in Maker, 1982, p. 81)

The generalizations students write at the end of a Concept Development lesson will be abstract enough to have broad application, yet complex enough to reveal the depth of conversation from which they emerged. It is the difference between:

Fruit is nutritious.
and
Fruit has a wide range of nutritional values, satisfying a variety of needs in the animal kingdom.

CHAPTER 3: TEACHING A CONCEPT DEVELOPMENT LESSON

In all cases it is important that the students perform the operations for themselves, see the relationships between items in their own way, ...and devise the categories or labels for the groups. The teacher should not do any of these things for them, although on rare occasions she might, if other methods fail, offer an alternative way of grouping items or even suggest that a list of items be extended. The important thing to aim for is a climate in which the teacher's suggestion is given no more status than that of the students'.... (Taba, Durkin, Fraenkel, & McNaughton, 1971, p. 69)

CONCEPT DEVELOPMENT WITH A WHOLE CLASS

Taba created her strategies when whole-class instruction was standard practice. While she incorporated small ways to increase individual student interaction (see Appendix C), she assumed that the majority of the lesson would take place with the entire class. This chapter follows Mr. Todd and his fourth-grade class as they work through a Concept Development lesson using this classic approach.

Today it is more common to vary classroom activity by incorporating time for students to work individually, in pairs, and in small groups. Chapter 4 features a Concept Development lesson that uses small-group work, along with discussion of how this changes the ebb and flow of the lesson.

STEP 1: LIST — TIME: 5 MINUTES

Goal:

- *Ask a focusing question that will help students create a list of about 25 items related to the discussion topic.*

Keys to Success:

- *Limit the list to about 25 items (15-25 for primary students).*
- *Ask focusing questions to ensure the list has proper breadth and reflects your Cognitive Map (see Chapter 5).*
- *Record student responses on the far left column of the chart.*
- *Break "chains" of responses by asking questions to refocus students' thinking.*
- *Be sure the list contains facts, not categories.*
- *Gather the entire list before asking the class to edit or remove items.*
- *Close the list before moving on to Step 2, Group and Label, by telling students that they cannot change or add any items for the remainder of the lesson.*

Listing lays the groundwork for the rest of the lesson, but even though it is important, it is not difficult. With proper preparation and effective focusing questions, it should be possible to move through this first step in a matter of minutes. Anything that gives students a moment to gather ideas will encourage participation and move the process along quickly. For example:

- After asking your first focusing question, have everyone write down two or three possible answers. Ask for their ideas round-robin style, asking everyone to contribute something from their list.

- Have students do a think-pair-share with a classmate after posing the first focusing question. Then have each pair contribute two ideas for the list.

- Provide the first focusing question for homework, and have each student think of three to five possible items (or pictures of them) to bring in the next day.

- Have pictures of items posted around the room or on a bulletin board ahead of time to prompt students' thinking.

- Call on quiet or typically reticent students early on to ensure full participation.

Starting the List. Mr. Todd has his board set up, his colored markers nearby, and his Cognitive Map and lesson plan (pp. 14-15) in hand. He's ready to start, so he asks the first focusing question from his lesson plan:

> *Mr. Todd:* *What are some examples of food we get from nature?*

He gives the students a minute to write down several ideas and tells them he wants one idea from each. As students respond, he writes the items on the far left-hand column of the board. As he goes around the room, he frequently asks students for the reasoning behind their choice. He also keeps his ears open so he can avoid possible problems.

Chained Responses. Very early in the conversation, students start a chain of responses. Allison suggests *peaches* for the list. The next three students offer:

Apples
Pineapples
Pears

This string of responses is a "chain." Chains begin when students build directly off of one idea. Some piggybacking of this sort is fine, but if the chain continues uninterrupted, the list will lack necessary breadth. After all, this is supposed to be a lesson about food from nature, not about fruit! Fortunately, Mr. Todd is ready with follow-up questions to help his students refocus their thinking to other areas:

> *Mr. Todd:* *You know so many kinds of fruit! But that's not all you eat! Let's broaden the list a bit. What is an example of another kind of food from nature?*

Later he might prompt them again with the comment:

> *Mr. Todd:* *You can think of food from nature anywhere in the world.*

Mr. Todd's refocusing question prompts students to consider a broader range of ideas. Notice that he doesn't ask: "What kind of meat do people eat?" If he refocuses that specifically, he's likely to get a group called *Meats* in the next step. The category is fine—but he wants the students to come up with it on their own, not because he planted the idea. He'll get specific if he has to, but he tries to start with more general questions that encourage students to shift without pushing them in a particular direction.

Staying Focused on Facts. After working halfway across the room, Simon offers *vegetables*. Vegetables are a category of food, not a kind of food, so Mr. Todd follows up:

Mr. Todd: *What is an example of a vegetable?*

Myles: *Carrots.*

Mr. Todd writes *carrots* on the list. This way, Mr. Todd avoids having a list that is made up of groups instead of facts. A list that is actually a set of groups at the beginning of the lesson can lead to difficulty later in the lesson when students start trying to fit both facts and categories into groups.

Items that Don't Fit the List. Despite his focusing question that specifically asks for food from nature, Sarah offers *donuts*.

Just what Mr. Todd had hoped to avoid! So he probes a little:

Mr. Todd: *Sarah, how are donuts food from nature?*

Sarah: *Well, all of the ingredients come from nature. Mixing them together doesn't make them NOT from nature.*

Mr. Todd writes *donuts* on the board, even though he really doesn't think it belongs. Then he quickly asks a refocusing question to keep *donuts* from becoming the first of a chain:

Mr. Todd: *What are different examples of food that comes from nature?*

It might seem unusual for Mr. Todd to write an item on the board when he thinks it is off the mark, but he's aware of what he's doing. He realizes:

1. While Sarah is not quite right, she's not altogether wrong.
2. Addressing the issue at that moment could interrupt the smooth, swift pace of gathering information.
3. Most importantly, he wants to create some distance between Sarah and the idea she suggested. When the list is finished, the class will review the list as a whole together. By that point, *donuts* will simply be an item on the list, not "Sarah's idea." The class will be able to analyze the appropriateness of the suggestion more objectively, and Sarah is less likely to take the criticism personally.

Donuts stays on the list, at least for the moment.

Closing the List. Everyone has made a contribution, creating a list with 26 different kinds of food. Before moving to the next step, Mr. Todd asks the class to review the 26 items:

> *Mr. Todd:* *Let's look at our list. Let me know if you think there are any items that do not belong or if there are items we need to change in some way.*

Brendan raises his hand and suggests that maybe *donuts* doesn't really fit. Mr. Todd summarizes Sarah's defense without mentioning her name:

> *Mr. Todd:* *How would you respond to the argument that a donut is a combination of foods from nature?*

> *Brendan:* *Yeah, but nothing else on the list is. Everything else is just one thing by itself.*

Mr. Todd puts the issue to a class vote, reminding students that the question isn't whether they like donuts, but whether donuts belong on this particular list. *Donuts* is removed from the board. While in this case Mr. Todd hoped someone would question whether *donuts* is appropriate, he *always* asks the class to review the list before moving on to grouping and labeling to increase their ownership of the list.

After checking to see if there are issues with any of the other items, Mr. Todd closes the list:

> *Mr. Todd:* *Okay, this is our list. No additions, deletions, or substitutions from this point on!*

LISTING

List			
1. Steak 2. Peaches 3. Apples 4. Pineapples 5. Pears 6. Ham 7. Green beans 8. Carrots 9. Celery 10. Rice 11. Wheat 12. Tomatoes 13. Salmon 14. Milk 15. Chicken 16. Cheese 17. Shrimp 18. Seaweed 19. Eggs 20. Yogurt 21. Potatoes 22. Honey 23. Beans 24. Oatmeal 25. Broccoli			

A "closed" list creates the conditions necessary for creative thinking later in the lesson. Allowing for substitutions or additions simply removes the need for students to stretch their minds later. The list is now done, and they are ready for Step 2: Group and Label.

STEP 2: GROUP AND LABEL TIME: 20-25 MINUTES

Goals:

- *Recognize attributes shared by items on the list.*
- *Form groups based on shared attributes.*
- *Create one- to three-word labels for the groups.*

Keys to Success:

- *Move to the second column, and change marker color.*
- *Give novice students a structure to follow: Requiring at least four groups with at least five items each (or four groups with our items each) is a good place to start.*

- *As students become familiar with the strategy, remove the structure.*
- *Group first, then label to help students keep their thinking open and flexible.*
- *Keep labels one to three words long in order to force students to find core ideas.*
- *Ask probing questions to encourage students to reveal their reasoning.*
- *Review Appendices A and B.*

During grouping and labeling, students: 1) look for common attributes among items on the list, 2) create groups based on those attributes, and 3) identify a one- or two-word label that describes the similarity.

Grouping. Mr. Todd's students have finished listing and are about to begin grouping and labeling. Mr. Todd changes marker colors and moves to the second section of the board, where he'll keep track of the groups as they form. He asks the focusing question he wrote for this step:

> *Mr. Todd:* *Which items could go together because they are alike in some way? Let's try to form four different groups with <u>at least</u> five items in each group.*

Why does Mr. Todd require a specific number of groups and items? His students are new to Concept Development, and he realizes they need additional support to guide their work. Without some rules in place, they may try to fit all of the items in one or two groups, virtually removing the opportunity to subsume later. Or they might create 12 groups with two items each, which will really create problems when they start regrouping. Giving students a required number of groups guarantees that they will engage in productive work, especially while they are first learning the strategy. Once everyone is familiar with the strategy, Mr. Todd will take away these guidelines because he recognizes that sometimes students gain valuable insight by finding a connection between just one to two items.

More important than the specific number of groups is the requirement that students place all of the items, or nearly all of the items, in a group. When students are new to the strategy it's reasonable to leave a little "wiggle room," allowing a few leftover items, but as time goes on, they should be held to the more challenging standard of finding a place for every item.

Group, then Label. The biggest challenge of this step is to try to resist the natural tendency to select a label and then search for items that fit. While seemingly efficient, this approach can block flexible thinking. Mr. Todd's class has just run into this dilemma. His students started by selecting the label *Fruit* and then, naturally, included all of the fruit on the list.

Fruit
Peaches
Apples
Pineapples
Pears

But they are one item short! No matter how hard they look, the students cannot find another fruit to put in the group. They hit a mental wall and want to give up on the group. Mr. Todd knows the real problem: the students have closed their minds around the label *Fruit,* and this is keeping them from thinking about other ways that these four items are alike. He erases the label and reminds them:

Mr. Todd: *These four items are fruit, but it may not be all they have in common. Erase the word "fruit" from your minds, and search for other similarities.*

Peaches
Apples
Pineapple
Pears

Freed from their commitment to the label, students find it easier to shift to another attribute that unites these items, and others as well. All of these fruit are found preserved in cans, as are many vegetables, so they decide on the label *Sometimes Stored.*

Sometimes Stored
Peaches
Apples
Pineapples
Pears
Green beans

By labeling *after* grouping, students keep their thinking open and flexible until all of the items are placed in groups.

Because they found a broader label, the students were able to place 21 items from their list in one of their four groups.

GROUPS BEFORE LABELING

List	*Group and Label*		
1. Steak 2. Peaches 3. Apples 4. Pineapples 5. Pears 6. Ham 7. Green beans 8. Carrots 9. Celery 10. Rice 11. Wheat 12. Tomatoes 13. Salmon 14. Milk 15. Chicken 16. Cheese 17. Shrimp 18. Seaweed 19. Eggs 20. Yogurt 21. Potatoes 22. Honey 23. Beans 24. Oatmeal 25. Broccoli	**Sometimes Stored** Peaches Apples Pineapples Pears Green beans 2) Steak Shrimp Ham Chicken Salmon 3) Rice Beans Potatoes Oatmeal Wheat 4) Carrots Celery Broccoli Seaweed Tomatoes		

Labeling. Having clustered the items into groups, the class turns to labeling. Mr. Todd's focusing question reminds the students that their labels have to be brief and to the point:

Mr. Todd: *What one- to three-word labels would best describe what these items share in common?*

Mr. Todd occasionally likes to linger on this step, helping students express their ideas concisely. He also enjoys hearing the labels his students select and listening to their thinking evolve as they discuss different options. He turns his attention to the items his students suggested were *Meat*:

Mr. Todd: *I wonder if we can find a label that would allow us to include more items from our list.*

He is met with blank stares, so he narrows the question a bit:

Mr. Todd: *What label would allow us to include eggs in this group?*

Brendan: Muscle Builders.

Mr. Todd: *Why do you think* Muscle Builders *would work as a label?*

Brendan: *Well, because they are all foods that we are told to eat to build strong muscles.*

Mr. Todd: *What do these items all have that give you those strong muscles?*

Maria: *Protein?*

Mr. Todd: *What other items could we include in this group if we used the label* Protein*?*

They end up with a group that includes many more items:

~~Meats~~ Protein
Steak
Shrimp
Ham
Chicken
Salmon
Cheese
Eggs

GROUPING AND LABELING

List	*Group and Label*		
1. Steak 2. Peaches 3. Apples 4. Pineapples 5. Pears 6. Ham 7. Green beans 8. Carrots 9. Celery 10. Rice 11. Wheat 12. Tomatoes 13. Salmon 14. Milk 15. Chicken 16. Cheese 17. Shrimp 18. Seaweed 19. Eggs 20. Yogurt 21. Potatoes 22. Honey 23. Beans 24. Oatmeal 25. Broccoli	**Sometimes Stored** Peaches Apples Pineapples Pears Green beans **~~Meat~~ Protein** Steak Shrimp Ham Chicken Salmon Cheese Eggs **Starch** Rice Beans Potatoes Oatmeal Wheat **Vegetables** Carrots Celery Broccoli Seaweed Tomatoes		

STEP 3: SUBSUME TIME: 10-15 MINUTES

Goals:

- *Identify items that could belong to more than one group (grades K-5).*
- *Identify groups that could fit under the heading of another group (grades 4-12).*
- *Build a hierarchy of ideas.*

Keys to Success:

- *Change marker color, and record answers in the third column on the chart.*
- *Have younger students try to find items that fit in more than one group.*
- *Have older students try to find groups that could become subsets of other groups.*
- *Build hierarchies by creating subsets within larger groups; do not merge.*
- *Ask students to justify their reasoning.*

Grouping and labeling automatically lift students toward abstract thinking because labels are inherently more abstract than the items they represent. During subsuming, students again move to a higher level of thinking as they figure out which items or groups can fit within another group.

Subsuming includes two sets of skills: the ability to cross-categorize individual items in different groups, and the ability to see that some whole groups can fit inside of other groups. Students acquire the ability to cross-categorize individual items first; before they have this skill, it is nearly impossible for students to see a hierarchy of groups. Teachers should choose their focus based on age group. While there are no hard and fast rules, these guidelines can be used as a starting point:

• Grades K-3:	• Focus on helping students find items in one group that could also belong in another group.
• Grades 4-8:	• Include subsuming groups under other groups.
• Grades 9 and above:	• Focus primarily on subsuming groups under other groups.

Mr. Todd teaches fourth grade, so he starts with some cross-categorizing, but he'll quickly move to building hierarchies. He begins with a group where he thinks his students will have easy success:

Mr. Todd: *Which item or items in the group* Vegetables *could also belong to another group?*

If necessary, he will narrow the question:

Mr. Todd: *Which item or items in the group* Vegetables *could also belong to* Sometimes Stored?

Sure enough, Sarah volunteers that *tomatoes* could belong to the group *Sometimes Stored* as well as the group *Vegetables*. Peter then points out that *ham* could also go there, too. Mr. Todd asks Peter to support his idea:

Mr. Todd: *Why do you think that ham goes in* Sometimes Stored?

Peter: *Well, sometimes I see it in cans, too.*

Mr. Todd: *I've seen those cans. I still wonder, though, what else happens to ham to preserve it?*

Peter: *They put salt on it.*

Mr. Todd: *Ah, who else has heard of salting, or "brining"?*

A third student suggests that *potatoes* could also go in the group *Vegetables*. Clearly the students understand that items can be cross-categorized. Mr. Todd moves on to subsuming one group under another group by asking:

> *Mr. Todd:* *Which groups and all of its items could fit under another group?*

The students struggle with this one but eventually see that each kind of vegetable in the *Vegetable* group could fit in *Sometimes Stored*. Mr. Todd asks them for support, and they name ways in which each vegetable is preserved.

Creating Higher-Order Labels

One disadvantage of putting a limit on the number of items and groups is that students don't have many options for subsuming. Even though he is pleased with his students' thinking and could leave out this step of the lesson, Mr. Todd still wants to push his students a little further by asking them to create a higher-level label that connects the groups they've created:

> *Mr. Todd:* *What label could we give a larger group that includes* Protein, Starch, *and* Vegetables? *Think about something different from* Food from Nature.

By adding this caveat at the end, he pushes the students' thinking in a new direction and keeps them from cycling back to their starting point.

> *Maria:* *Well, we eat them all, so we could just call them* Eating Things.
>
> *Ethan:* *That's the same as calling them food, so we could just call them* Food.
>
> *Mr. Todd:* *Let's think about that. Why do we eat them all?*
>
> *Sarah:* *Because they're good for us.*
>
> *Mr. Todd:* *Why don't we eat just one?*
>
> *Peter:* *Because they give us something different.*
>
> *Mr. Todd:* *I hear you saying that they are all good for us, and each group gives us something different. How can we put those two ideas together to create a label?*
>
> *Maria:* Most Food Needs.
>
> *Mr. Todd:* *Class, how many of you think this works as a label for* Starch, Vegetables, *and* Protein?

The class votes to approve this label.

SUBSUMING

List	*Group and Label*	*Subsuming*	
1. Steak	**Sometimes Stored**		
2. Peaches	Peaches	**Sometimes Stored**	
3. Apples	Apples	*Tomatoes*	
4. Pineapples	Pineapple	*Ham*	
5. Pears	Pears	*Vegetables*	
6. Ham	Green beans		
7. Green beans			
8. Carrots	**~~Meat~~ Protein**		
9. Celery	Steak		
10. Rice	Shrimp		
11. Wheat	Ham	**Most Food Needs**	
12. Tomatoes	Chicken	*Starch*	
13. Salmon	Salmon	*Protein*	
14. Milk	Cheese	*Vegetables*	
15. Chicken	Eggs		
16. Cheese			
17. Shrimp	**Starch**		
18. Seaweed	Rice		
19. Eggs	Beans		
20. Yogurt	Potatoes		
21. Potatoes	Oatmeal		
22. Honey	Wheat		
23. Beans			
24. Oatmeal	**Vegetables**		
25. Broccoli	Carrots		
	Celery		
	Broccoli		
	Seaweed		
	Tomatoes		

Summarize before Proceeding. Summarizing at this point is not a formal part of the Concept Development strategy, but taking a minute for students to gather their thoughts now prepares them to write generalizations at the end of the lesson. Pause for a moment, and ask the students for one or two statements that summarize what they have learned so far. When Mr. Todd asks this question, the students first repeat that most food can be preserved. Others then add that food comes in lots of varieties, and different foods serve different purposes, but they all make us healthy.

STEP IV: REGROUPING — TIME: 20-25 MINUTES

Goals:

- *Encourage original, divergent thinking.*
- *Create conditions for abstract thinking.*

Keys to Success:

- *Change marker color, and record work in the fourth column on the chart.Introduce the step with upbeat energy and enthusiasm.*
- *Remind students they must create new groups; they cannot reuse or rename groups.*
- *If necessary, reduce the number of required groups and/or the number of items in the groups to modulate the level of challenge.*
- *Refocus student thinking as needed to remind them of the variety of ways items on the list can be viewed, used, or interpreted.*

During grouping and labeling, students often cluster items together using fairly obvious attributes. During regrouping, the first groups and labels are put off limits so students have to search for unusual, original relationships. With fewer easy answers to rely on, regrouping is significantly more challenging than grouping and labeling; students often need more support and encouragement (see The Emotional Tempo of Concept Development on p. 37). As students stretch to see new relationships, they also tend to find more abstract ideas; labels created at this stage are more likely to be creative, abstract, or conceptual than the first set of labels.

Introducing Regrouping. Mr. Todd knows he has to be upbeat and positive while introducing this next stage, communicating in word and deed that he has every expectation that his students will produce wonderful new groups.

> *Mr. Todd:* *Wow! You've done such a great job with this that I think we should go on! Let's make some entirely NEW groups. You can reuse items, but you can't use a group that's already been used or simply rename an existing group.*

He tells students that their goal is to identify *three new groups* with at least *four items each*. He decreases the total number of groups to balance the level of challenge and the quantity students have to produce.

Despite the upbeat cheerleading, the students groan. AGAIN? They seem a bit sulky. Mr. Todd is not concerned; he knows this is just a sign that the students are stuck. They're having trouble seeing beyond the groups they've already created and are putting up some resistance to changing their thinking. But he keeps propping his students up with his energy, modeling the attitude that will help them open their minds to new possibilities. Before long, the students are getting excited again.

The first cluster they create includes *eggs, cheese, honey,* and *yogurt*, suggesting the label Animal Gifts. Then they try to find a group of food from trees but can only find three items: *peaches*, *apples*, and *pears*. Next they try grouping:

Celery
Potatoes
Tomatoes
Carrots
Broccoli

Mr. Todd steps in:

Mr. Todd: *I see a group on the board already with all of these items—how is this a new group?*

Sheepishly, the students give up on the idea but pretty quickly form a group of *pineapples*, *carrots*, *celery*, and *potatoes* which they call *Ground Grown*. Then the class grows quiet; they seem to have run out of ideas. Mr. Todd waits patiently, realizing that the best ideas often emerge after a pause in activity. He reads the remaining items aloud. Vinny suggests clustering shrimp, salmon, and seaweed, but he can't figure out a fourth item that relates to seafood. Mr. Todd reminds the class that twice already in this lesson they were able to get past rough spots by broadening their thinking. Then he asks:

Mr. Todd: *What else on our list is grown in water?*

Alex: *Rice!*

Shrimp, *rice*, *seaweed*, and *salmon* become the group *Water-Based*.

Mr. Todd asks the class to review the groups and labels to see if there is anything they want to change. He asks students for clarification about the meaning of the label *Animal Gifts* and finds he's not the only one who found this label unclear.

Sarah: *Yeah, chickens don't lay eggs for us as presents; they lay eggs to make little chickens.*

Alex: *How about* Animals Make*?*

Mr. Todd: *What are some other words for "make"?*

Students offer:

Build
Produce
Create

After discussing these options, they settle on *Animals Produce*. Students are ready for the final part of the lesson.

REGROUPING

List	*Group and Label*	*Subsume*	*Regroup*
1. Steak	**Sometimes Stored**	**Sometimes Stored**	
2. Peaches	Peaches	*Tomatoes*	**Animals Produce**
3. Apples	Apples	*Ham*	Eggs
4. Pineapples	Pineapples	*Vegetables*	Cheese
5. Pears	Pears		Honey
6. Ham	Green beans		Yogurt
7. Green beans		**Starch**	Milk
8. Carrots	**~~Meat~~ Protein**	*Rice*	
9. Celery	Steak	*Wheat*	
10. Rice	Shrimp	*Oatmeal*	
11. Wheat	Ham	*Beans*	**Ground Grown-Farmed**
12. Tomatoes	Chicken	*Potatoes*	
13. Salmon	Salmon		Pineapples
14. Milk	Chees		Carrots
15. Chicken	Eggs	**Most Food Needs**	Celery
16. Cheese		*Protein*	Potatoes
17. Shrimp	**Starch**	*Starch*	
18. Seaweed	Rice	*Vegetables*	
19. Eggs	Beans		
20. Yogurt	Potatoes		**Water-Based**
21. Potatoes	Oatmeal		Salmon
22. Honey	Wheat		Shrimp
23. Beans			Seaweed
24. Oatmeal	**Vegetables**		Rice
25. Broccoli	Carrots		
	Celery		
	Broccoli		
	Seaweed		
	Tomatoes		
	Potatoes		

STEP V: GENERALIZE TIME: 15 MINUTES

Goal:
- *Create generalizations that express abstract ideas based on the conversation.*

Keys to Success:
- *Change marker color, and move to a new section of the board.*
- *Include cues in your focusing question that refer students back to the conversation to make their generalizations.*
- *After posing focusing questions, give students time to write ideas down or think-pair-share.*
- *Make sure students use information from the conversation to justify their statements.*

The ultimate purpose of Concept Development is to have students work with a set of facts to find ways that reveal the big ideas that unify them, so it's only natural that students are asked to write generalizations at the end of a Concept Development lesson. Mr. Todd has been using the Concept Development strategy for a few years, so he is aware of the need to prepare his students for this next step. If he simply asks them, "What are some general statements we can make about the food we eat?" he might get overly broad, superficial catch-phrases that aren't really connected to the discussion. So he asks the focusing question carefully:

Mr. Todd:	*Based on our list and all of the groups and labels we've made, what are some general statements we can make about humans, nature, and food?*

By using this phrasing, Mr. Todd makes it clear that he only wants statements that *connect* to the conversation, not platitudes like "Food is good for you," or "Always eat your vegetables." After giving the students a minute of quiet time to think and scribble an idea on scrap paper, he asks them to share their ideas, making sure to thank the first person who volunteers, since students can be hesitant to risk being "wrong" at this step. As usual, he writes down several ideas on the board before working with any of them:

Humans preserve food from nature.

Humans grow or get food from nature.

Nature creates a variety of food that humans eat.

With this list on the board, he steps back, considers the list, and then turns to the class.

Mr. Todd:	*Let's take the phrases "Humans preserve food from nature" and "Humans grow or get food from nature." How can we combine those into a single statement?*
Brendan:	*We can combine them: "Humans gather, grow, and preserve food from nature."*
Mr. Todd:	*Class, what do you think?*

The class agrees that this is an improvement, so Mr. Todd moves to the last statement:

Mr. Todd:	*Now let's look at "Nature creates a variety of food that humans eat" and clarify this a little. Why do we eat a variety of food from nature?*
Vinny:	*We would die if we didn't.*

Mr. Todd:	*We would die. What would happen before we died if we just stopped eating?*
Shane:	*Well, we'd get hungry and sick.*
Mr. Todd:	*So how could we revise this statement to make it a complete idea?*
Allison:	*Add "to stay healthy and alive" at the end.*

Mr. Todd makes the correction, and they end the lesson with two generalizations:

Humans gather, grow, and preserve food from nature.

Nature creates a variety of food that humans eat to stay healthy and alive.

The students are beginning to get a glazed look, and Mr. Todd knows it's time to stop. He wraps up the lesson by assigning some students the job of writing this generalization on a large strip of paper. That piece of paper will go above the whiteboard so that, as the students continue their studies, they can refer back to the idea, editing and revising as their understanding evolves. This way, the generalization becomes a working tool for the students to use, rather than an inert, abstract statement.

At the end of the day, Mr. Todd compares the board his class created to his Cognitive Map (p. 15). As always, the list the students created was a bit different from his. Some of the items he was ready to ask them about, like raisins and peanuts, didn't emerge. Even so, the groups were fairly similar, and the final ideas students created were comparable to the ones he hoped they would see. Most importantly, the ideas came from the students, not from him.

Over the next couple of days, Mr. Todd will continue to work on the ideas that emerged during the lesson. For example, he will have the students create a bulletin board tree map using the categories they created during the Concept Development lesson. He will also use a follow-up Taba strategy, Concept Attainment, to help the students test their generalizations by asking them to find a food that does not come from nature.

The Emotional Tempo of Concept Development

The Concept Development strategy has an emotional tempo as well as an intellectual tempo. The first steps generally evoke high-energy engagement. Students usually don't find the first round too difficult and enjoy the opportunity to work out the puzzle of getting everything sorted. Labeling and subsuming are a bit harder, and you will feel the energy of the room change as you push them to more precision in discussion of labels and more abstraction during subsuming.

During regrouping, the emotional energy of the classroom often changes from enjoyment and excitement to concentration and intensity or, sometimes, to frustration. Teachers are sometimes distressed by this shift in energy, but it is a very productive change. This is a sign that you are presenting students with a true challenge, pushing them to new and different kinds of thinking. You and your students will find that while the effort is harder at this step of the lesson, the results are more original and the sense of satisfaction much greater in the end.

FINISHED LESSON

List	*Group and Label*	*Subsume*	*Regroup*
1. Steak	**Sometimes Stored**	**Sometimes Stored**	**~~Animal Gifts~~**
2. Peaches	Peaches	*Tomatoes*	**Animals Produce**
3. Apples	Apples	*Ham*	Cheese
4. Pineapples	Pineapples	*Vegetables*	Eggs
5. Pears	Pears		Honey
6. Ham	Green beans		Yogurt
7. Green beans			Milk
8. Carrots	**~~Meat~~ Protein**		
9. Celery	Steak	**Most Food Needs**	
10. Rice	Shrimp	*Protein*	
11. Wheat	Ham	*Starch*	**Ground Grown**
12. Tomatoes	Chicken	*Vegetables*	**Farmed**
13. Salmon	Salmon		Pineapples
14. Milk	Cheese		Carrots
15. Chicken	Eggs		Celery
16. Cheese			Potatoes
17. Shrimp	**Starch**		
18. Seaweed	Rice		
19. Eggs	Beans		
20. Yogurt	Potatoes		**Water-Based**
21. Potatoes	Oatmeal		Salmon
22. Honey	Wheat		Shrimp
23. Beans			Seaweed
24. Oatmeal	**Vegetables**		Rice
25. Broccoli	Carrots		
	Celery		
	Broccoli		
	Seaweed		
	Tomatoes		

Generalizations: *Humans gather, grow, and preserve food from nature. Nature creates a variety of food that humans eat to stay healthy and alive.*

SUMMARY: THE FIVE STAGES OF CONCEPT DEVELOPMENT

Step	*Goals*	*Keys to Success*
Step 1: ***List***	*Help students create a list of about 25 items similar to the list on your Cognitive Map.*	*Keep the list at about 25 items (15-25 for primary students).* *Ask focusing questions to ensure the list has proper breadth and reflects your Cognitive Map.* *Record student responses on the far left column of the chart.* *Break "chains" of responses by refocusing students' thinking.* *Be sure the list contains facts, not categories.* *Gather the list; then ask the class to edit or remove items as appropriate.* *Close the list before moving on to grouping and labeling by telling students that they cannot change or add any items for the remainder of the lesson.*
Step 2: ***Group and Label***	*Recognize attributes shared by items on the list.* *Form groups based on shared attributes.* *Create one- to three-word labels for the groups.*	*Move to the second column, and change marker color for this step.* *Give novice students a structure to follow. Requiring at least five groups with at least four items each is a good place to start.* *As students become familiar with the strategy, remove the structure.* *Group first, then label to help students keep their thinking open and flexible.* *Keep labels one to three words long to force students to find core ideas.* *Ask probing questions to encourage students to reveal their reasoning.*
Step 3: ***Subsume***	*Identify items that could belong to more than one group (grades K-5).* *Identify groups that could fit under the heading of another group (grades 4-12).* *Build a hierarchy of ideas.*	*Change marker color, and record work in the third column on the chart.* *Have younger students try to find items that fit in more than one group.* *Have older students try to find groups that could become subsets of other groups.* *Build hierarchies by creating subsets within larger groups; do not merge.* *If desired, ask students to create new, higher-order labels that unite current groups.* *Ask students to justify their reasoning.*

Step 4: ***Regroup***	*Encourage original, divergent thinking.* *Create conditions for abstract thinking.*	*Change marker color, and record work in the fourth column on the chart.* *Introduce the step with upbeat energy and enthusiasm.* *Remind students they must create new groups; they cannot reuse or rename groups.* *If necessary, reduce the number of required groups and/or the number of items in the groups to modulate the level of challenge.* *Refocus student thinking as needed to remind them of the variety of ways items on the list can be viewed, used, or interpreted.*
Step 5: ***Generalize***	*Create generalizations that express abstract ideas based on the conversation.*	*Change marker color, and move to a new section of the board.* *Include cues in your focusing question that refer students back to the conversation to make their generalizations.* *After posing focusing questions, give students time to write ideas down or think-pair-share.* *Make sure students use information from the conversation to justify their statements.*

PRACTICE

Exercise 1: Turn back to Mr. Todd's Cognitive Map on page 15, and compare it to the final chart created by Mr. Todd and his students during the lesson (p. 37).

What differences do you see?

____

____

____

How important are these differences to the outcome of the lesson?

____

____

____

Exercise 2: Think of three different ways to ask each question. Keep your questions open-ended!

a. "What is an example of a vegetable?"

____

____

____

b. "Why do you think so?"

____

____

____

Exercise 3: Try to write two open-ended questions to help students:

Clarify their group labels.

____

____

Subsume groups instead of merging groups.

____

____

Exercise 4: Reflect: What would have happened to the lesson if the item *donut* had stayed on the list? What are the advantages or disadvantages of having that item stay on the list?

____

____

____

____

____

____

____

____

____

CHAPTER 4: VARIATIONS ON CONCEPT DEVELOPMENT: MIDDLE AND HIGH SCHOOL

> *If a teacher is having trouble with the Concept Development task, the first thing he should analyze is the opening question. Is it the type of question that will get out the needed data and get as many students as possible to respond early in the discussion?* (Taba, Durkin, Fraenkel, & McNaughton, 1971, p.162)

Chapter 3 contained a detailed description of an entire class working together on a Concept Development lesson. This chapter presents examples of how to modify the strategy. The examples are not as detailed, focusing primarily on how the variations affect the flow of a Concept Development lesson. In the first example, a middle school teacher integrates small-group work into a Concept Development lesson. In the second example, a high school teacher spreads the Concept Development lesson over three days, using a homework assignment as a bridge.

CONCEPT DEVELOPMENT IN SEVENTH- GRADE SCIENCE

Ms. Marshall has discussed the concept of *systems* in her science classes from the beginning of the year, but she is not satisfied that her students really understand the connection between the concept and the natural world. She has decided to use Concept Development to help her classes extend their understanding of systems, specifically about interactions in a prairie ecosystem. Ms. Marshall introduced her students to the short grass prairie through a WebQuest investigation of the endangered black-footed ferret. Having gathered information from a variety of articles, each focusing on a different aspect of the problem, Ms. Marshall's students now need a way to organize what they've learned.

PREPARING FOR THE LESSON

Ms. Marshall likes an active classroom, not only because it suits her personal style, but also because she knows that variety is a key to success with middle school students. She will build two opportunities for small-group work in her Concept Development lesson: during grouping and labeling and again during regrouping. With opportunities to go back and forth from whole-group to small-group work, she feels she has the right combination to keep her 90 minute block-scheduled class dynamic. She prepares materials in advance to ensure smooth transitions from whole-class discussion to small-group activity. Her preparations include:

1) Completing a Cognitive Map for the lesson (see pp. 45-46). The Cognitive Map is particularly useful for this lesson because the topic has so many different dimensions. Thinking through the Cognitive Map helps Ms. Marshall identify which areas are particularly important.

2) Creating task cards with instructions for grouping and labeling and regrouping, one set for each table of students (pp. 49, 54).

3) Assigning her class tables with about five students each.

4) Distributing sets of blank index cards or Post-It notes for each table. Ms. Marshall tells each table to select someone to write one item on each. She emphasizes that their cards should have the same items as

the list going up on the butcher paper—they can't use different items at their table!

5) Taping four pieces of butcher paper on the wall. If the students are not finished with the lesson by the end of class, she will simply take them down, roll them up, and save them for the next day. Ms. Marshall likes her system of keeping the charts for each of her four sections of science in the corner; with help from her students, she switches sets quickly between classes.

6) Gathering colored markers so that each step can be recorded on the butcher paper in a different color.

7) Asking one student from each group to serve as "scribe" to record class notes on the butcher paper. Each scribe is responsible for a different step of the lesson so they don't spend the whole class period writing.

Lesson Plan: *Concept Development*
Grade Level: *Secondary*
Purpose of Discussion: *To extend and clarify students' understanding of a prairie ecosystem*
Background Information for Lesson: *WebQuest on endangered black-footed ferret*

Concept Development	*Focusing Questions*	*Materials and Supports*
Step 1: List	*What facts did you find related to the endangered black-footed ferrets?* *What did you find other than issues involving breeding ferrets?*	• WebQuest research previous day with note-taking guide • Butcher paper on the wall and colored markers • Index cards/Post-its for student groups
Step 2: Group and Label	Grouping (as on task card): *Some of the facts on your cards share common characteristics or attributes. See if you can gain new insight about the problem by grouping these facts based on a common attribute or on something they have in common.* Labeling: *We have two labels for the group (x). Which seems to be the most accurate description? Why?*	• Task cards • Short time limit • Change colored markers. • Have tables report groups round-robin style, asking for new and unique groups. • Remember to ask for multiple ideas. • Ask for justification for each label.
Step 3: Subsume	*Which group could fit under another group? What makes you think (x) fits inside (y)?* or *What group could fit inside (ecosystem interactions)? Why do you think so?* Quick Summary Question: *Based on our list, groups, and hierarchy, what insights are emerging about the black-footed ferret's ecosystem?*	• Change marker colors; use third column. • Show hierarchy by listing in outline form on the board.
Step 4: Regroup	As on task card: *Now it's time to STRETCH!* *Create three completely new groups that bring insight to our topic. The groups can have any number of items, but you can't use any item twice. After you've created your groups, decide on a label.*	• Change marker colors; use fourth column. • Report round-robin style again.
Step 5: Generalize	*Thinking about our entire conversation, including the list, all of our groups and labels, and the hierarchy we created by subsuming groups, what general statements can we make about the prairie ecosystem?*	• Give students a minute of individual think time to write down ideas before discussing as a class. • Start with one idea, and have others integrate their ideas into the first.

Lesson Plan: <u>Concept Development</u>
Cognitive Map: Black Footed Ferret and Ecosystems

Possible List	*Possible Groups and Labels*		*Possible Subsuming*
1. Ferrets live in prairie dog holes 2. Ferrets are the most endangered mammal in North America 3. Ranchers think prairie dogs holes hurt cows 4. Cheatgrass is invading the prairie 5. A ferret eats 100 prairie dogs/year 6. Prairie dogs have been shot and poisoned 7. Prairie dogs, ferrets can get plague 8. Pets can get plague from prairie dogs 9. Most of the ferret diet is prairie dog 10. Ferrets have a genetic bottleneck 11. Scientists have bred ferrets in captivity to save them 12. Cows don't break legs in prairie dog holes 13. Prairie dogs are a keystone species 14. Ferrets have about four kits in a litter 15. Prairie dog digging helps natural prairie grasses grow 16. Farmers are afraid that prairie dogs eat the grass cows need 17. Cheatgrass increases fire risk to the prairie 18. Ranchers shoot prairie dogs for sport 19. Cows and bison like to eat near prairie dog burrows 20. A genetic bottleneck means that there is not enough variation in DNA to survive as a species 21. Lack of variation in DNA makes ferrets physically fragile (kidneys) 22. Younger released ferrets survive longer than older ferrets 23. Ferrets were thought extinct; the last group was discovered by a dog 24. Coyotes, owls, eagles, badgers eat ferrets 25. Breeding ferrets is expensive and has had limited success	**<u>Ferret Life</u>** A ferret eats 100 prairie dogs/year Most of the ferret diet is prairie dog Ferrets have about four kits in a litter Coyotes, owls, eagles, badgers eat ferrets **<u>Ferret Endangered</u>** Ferrets are the most endangered mammal in North America Ferrets have a genetic bottleneck Scientists have bred ferrets in captivity to save them A genetic bottleneck means that there is not enough variation in DNA to survive as a species Ferrets were thought extinct, the last group were discovered by a dog Breeding ferrets is expensive and has had limited success Younger released ferrets survive longer than older ferrets	**<u>Ecosystem Interactions</u>** Ferrets live in prairie dog holes Coyotes, owls, eagles, badgers eat ferrets Cows and bison like to eat near prairie dog burrows Cheatgrass is invading the prairie Prairie dogs are a keystone species **<u>Risks</u>** Prairie dogs have been shot and poisoned by local farmers Prairie dogs, ferrets can get plague Cheatgrass increases fire risk to the prairie Lack of variation in DNA makes ferrets physically fragile (kidneys) **<u>Prairie Dogs Involved</u>** Ranchers think prairie dog holes hurt cows Ranchers shoot prairie dogs for sport Prairie dog digging helps natural prairie grasses grow A ferret eats 100 prairie dogs/year Prairie dogs are a keystone species	**<u>Ferret Life</u>** **<u>Ferret Endangered</u>** **<u>Risks</u>** **<u>Ecosystem Interactions</u>** **<u>Prairie Dogs Involved</u>** ***Possible Regrouping*** **<u>Human Fears</u>** Pets get plague from prairie dog Ranchers think prairie dogs holes hurt cows Farmers are afraid that prairie dogs eat the grass cows need **<u>Prairie Problems</u>** Prairie dogs, ferrets can get plague Cheatgrass is invading the prairie Prairie dogs have been shot and poisoned

Possible Generalizations (Step 5): The prairie ecosystem is dependent on keystone species. Ecosystems are interdependent.

STEP 1: LISTING TIME: 5 MINUTES

Even when incorporating small-group work into Concept Development, it is best to develop the initial list as an entire class. This ensures that everyone: 1) helps to create the list, 2) uses the same list to create groups, and 3) agrees to the meaning of the items. Ms. Marshall knows that her students have a lot of information on their research notes, so she starts gathering items for the list by asking the focusing question:

What facts help explain why the black-footed ferret is endangered?

She watches as the list of items grows on the first piece of butcher paper, keeping track to make sure all of the general areas on her Cognitive Map are represented. As necessary, she asks follow-up questions, including:

- *How does (x) contribute to the ferret's problem?*
- *What effect does (x) have on the ferret's survival?*

She also asks questions to broaden the list, such as:

- *Who has a fact that is not directly related to the ferret but still affects its survival?*
- *What other aspects of the ferret's life or environment seem to contribute to the problem?*
- *Who has a fact that is similar to, but not the same as, this one?*

When finished, the class can see the compiled list on butcher paper; each table also has a collection of index cards that they can begin to sort into groups (Figure 1, p. 50).

CLASS RECORD OF CONCEPT DEVELOPMENT LESSON ON BLACK-FOOTED FERRET AND ECOSYSTEMS LISTING

List	*Group and Label*	*Subsume*
1. Ranchers think prairie dog holes hurt cows		
2. Cheatgrass is invading prairie		
3. Ferrets live in prairie dog holes		
4. Ferrets are endangered		
5. A ferret eats 100 prairie dogs/year		
6. Prairie dogs are almost wiped out		
7. Prairie dogs, ferrets can get plague		
8. Ferret diet is 95% prairie dog		
9. Ferrets have a genetic bottleneck		
10. Cows don't break legs in prairie dog holes		*Regroup*
11. Reintroducing ferrets has been hard		
12. Prairie dogs are a keystone species		
13. There are 3-4 kits in a ferret litter		
14. Prairie dog digging helps natural prairie grasses grow		
15. Cheatgrass increases brush fire hazard		
16. Ranchers "plink" (shoot) prairie dogs for sport		
17. Cows and bison like to eat near prairie dog burrows		
18. Limited DNA has made ferrets fragile		
19. Ferrets are bred in captivity and released		
20. Ranchers killed most prairie dogs		
21. Ferrets can get canine distemper		
22. Ferrets were thought extinct until Shep (dog) found one		
23. Coyotes, owls, eagles, badgers eat ferrets		
24. Climate is changing prairie into desert		
25. Ferret survival tied to prairie dog		

STEP 2: GROUPING AND LABELING IN SMALL GROUPS 20-25 MINUTES

Grouping. Ms. Marshall gives each table a task card with instructions for grouping and labeling. She has found that using task cards reduces the number of times she has to repeat instructions. As usual, she gives her students a tight timeline to encourage focused work; if they work hard and still don't finish, she'll extend the time limit.

Students shift the cards around on their table; this gives them a concrete sense of how their thoughts are taking shape. When the time is up, many groups have their cards sorted into piles or laid out in lines on their desks. Ms. Marshall asks the class to bring their attention to the front of the room again so they can start sharing their ideas.

Reporting Groups. Five tables of students working independently will naturally take different approaches to grouping the items, so there will be more groups to discuss. It helps to have an efficient method for sharing their work. Ms. Marshall goes round-robin from table to table, asking each table to offer a group that is different from the groups already on the board. She continues working around the room, accepting only new and different groupings until are all listed on the board. She instructs the scribe for this step to record groups and labels; if another table clustered the same items but gave them different labels, the different labels are recorded. Discussion is held until all ideas have been collected.

Grouping and Labeling Task Card:
Some of the facts on your cards share common characteristics, or *attributes*. See if you can gain new insight about the ferret's ecosystem by grouping these facts based on a common attribute, or on something they have in common. Here are your guidelines:

- Create **five groups** with *at least* **four items** each.
- Each item should be used *only once!*
- Keep your thinking loose!!! Cluster your facts into groups first; *then* think about labels.
- Assign a one-word label for your groups. You may treat "prairie dog" as one word.

You have **FIVE MINUTES** to finish this task.

FIGURE 1: GROUPING ITEMS WITH INDEX CARDS

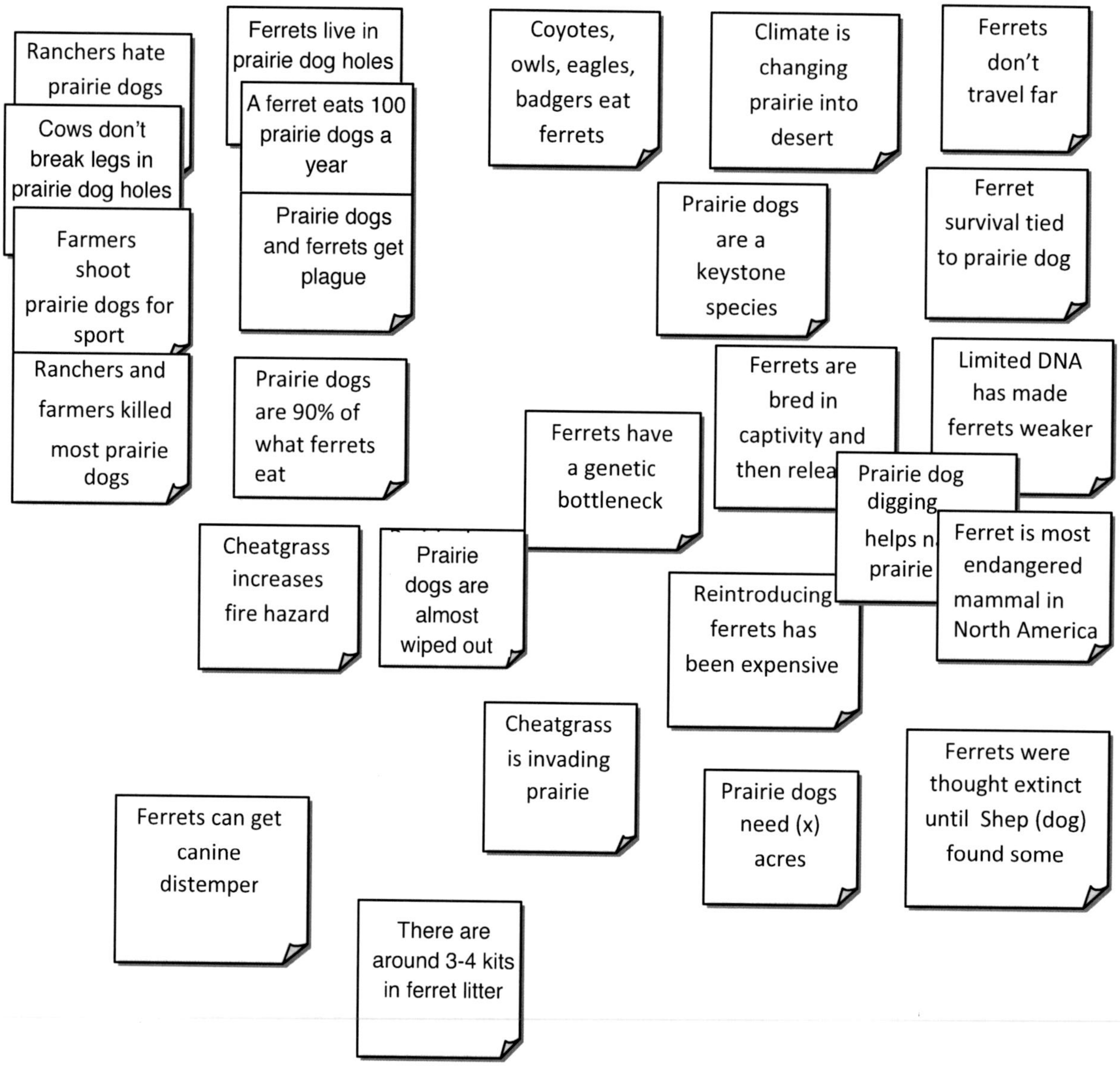

CLASS RECORD OF CONCEPT DEVELOPMENT LESSON ON BLACK- FOOTED FERRET AND ECOSYSTEMS WITH GROUPS AND LABELS

List	*Group and Label*		*Subsume* / *Regroup*
1. Ranchers think prairie dog holes hurt cows 2. Cheatgrass is invading prairie 3. Ferrets live in prairie dog holes 4. Ferrets are endangered 5. A ferret eats 100 prairie dogs/year 6. Prairie dogs are almost wiped out 7. Prairie dogs, ferrets can get plague 8. Ferret diet is 95% prairie dog 9. Ferrets have a genetic bottleneck 10. Cows don't break legs in prairie dog holes 11. Reintroducing ferrets has been hard 12. Prairie dogs are a keystone species 13. There are 3-4 kits in a ferret litter 14. Prairie dog digging helps natural prairie grasses grow 15. Cheatgrass increases brush fire hazard 16. Ranchers "plink" (shoot) prairie dogs for sport 17. Cows and bison like to eat near prairie dog burrows 18. Limited DNA has made ferrets fragile 19. Ferrets are bred in captivity and released 20. Ranchers killed most prairie dogs 21. Ferrets can get canine distemper 22. Ferrets were thought extinct until Shep (dog) found one 23. Coyotes, owls, eagles, badgers eat ferrets 24. Climate is changing prairie into desert 25. Ferret survival tied to prairie dog	**~~Humans~~ Rancher Influence ~~Human Influence~~** Ranchers think prairie dogs holes hurt cows Cows don't break legs in prairie dog holes Ranchers "plink" prairie dogs Ranchers have killed most prairie dogs **~~Ferrets~~ Ferret Facts** Ferrets are endangered Ferrets have a genetic bottleneck Reintroducing ferrets has been hard There are 3-4 kits in a ferret litter Limited DNA has made ferrets fragile Ferrets are bred in captivity and released Ferrets can get canine distemper Ferrets were thought extinct until Shep (dog) found one Coyotes, owls, eagles, badgers eat ferrets **Prairie Dogs** Prairie dogs are almost wiped out Prairie dogs are a keystone species Prairie dogs need (x) acres to live Prairie dogs, ferrets can get plague **Sharing Land ~~Animal Territories~~** Ferrets live in prairie dog holes Cows don't break legs in prairie dog holes Prairie dog digging helps natural prairie grasses grow Cows and bison like to eat near prairie dog burrows	**~~Environment~~ Environmental Threat** Cheatgrass is invading prairie Cheatgrass increases brush fire hazard Climate is changing prairie into desert. Prairie is overgrazed **~~Ferrets and Prairie Dogs~~ Prairie Dog Importance** Ferrets live in prairie dog burrows A ferret eats 100 prairie dogs/year Ferret diet is 90% prairie dog Ferret survival tied to prairie dog **Ferret Threats** Cheatgrass increases brush fire hazard Ranchers "plink" prairie dogs Ferrets can get canine distemper Ferrets have genetic bottleneck Coyotes, owls, eagles, badgers eat ferrets **Recovery Challenges** Ferrets are endangered Ferrets have a genetic bottleneck There are 3-4 kits in a litter Prairie dogs are almost wiped out Ferret recovery has been expensive **~~Outside~~ Indirect Changes** Cheatgrass is invading prairie Climate is changing prairie into desert Ranchers "plink" (shoot) prairie dogs for sport Prairie dogs are almost wiped out	

Labeling.

As expected, several of the groups on the board have more than one label. Ms. Marshall wants to help her students refine their thinking and find the label that is really a best fit for each group.

She starts with a group on the board that one table labeled *Humans*, but other tables labeled *Human Influence* and another table labeled *Rancher Influence.*

<u>*Humans*</u>
Ranchers think prairie dog holes hurt cows
Cows don't break legs in prairie dog holes
Ranchers "plink" prairie dogs
Ranchers have killed most prairie dogs

Ms. Marshall opens the floor to a brief discussion. The class sees right away that one-word labels are too broad to describe the unique features of a group. After discussing the ideas behind each of the suggestions, the class agrees that *Rancher Influence* describes the list best. Then Ms. Marshall asks about the label: *Ferrets and Prairie Dogs*. The students balk a bit, insisting that the relationship between ferrets and prairie dogs is essential to the topic. Ms. Marshall asks the students to identify which animal is the central focus of the group. The students acknowledge that the prairie dog is the real subject of the group, and someone suggests that *Prairie Dog Importance* is more descriptive of the items.

STEP 3: SUBSUME 10-15 MINUTES

Students working at tables will construct groups somewhat differently, so many individual items are already cross-categorized across the groups listed on the board. Ms. Marshall makes note of interesting cross-referenced items but quickly turns the students' attention to building hierarchies with groups. She asks her students to identify which whole group could be a subset of another, broader group. Subsuming tends to be a little easier when there are several groups to work with; students may even find multi-layered hierarchies using whole groups. Ms. Marshall's class does a fast job of organizing the first set of groups into categories and sub-categories—they've read enough articles that they can structure the ideas without too much trouble. She's glad of this because she wanted to spend more time on the next step, where she thinks the lesson will have its best learning value.

CLASS RECORD OF CONCEPT DEVELOPMENT LESSON ON BLACK FOOTED FERRET AND ECOSYSTEMS WITH SUBSUMING

List	*Group and Label*		*Subsume*
1. Ranchers think prairie dog holes hurt cows 2. Cheatgrass is invading prairie 3. Ferrets live in prairie dog holes 4. Ferrets are endangered 5. A ferret eats 100 prairie dogs/year 6. Prairie dogs are almost wiped out 7. Prairie dogs, ferrets can get plague 8. Ferret diet is 95% prairie dog 9. Ferrets have a genetic bottleneck 10. Cows don't break legs in prairie dog holes 11. Reintroducing ferrets has been hard 12. Prairie dogs are a keystone species 13. There are 3-4 kits in a ferret litter 14. Prairie dog digging helps natural prairie grasses grow 15. Cheatgrass increases brush fire hazard 16. Ranchers "plink" (shoot) prairie dogs for sport 17. Cows and bison like to eat near prairie dog burrows 18. Limited DNA has made ferrets fragile 19. Ferrets are bred in captivity and released 20. Ranchers killed most prairie dogs 21. Ferrets can get canine distemper 22. Ferrets were thought extinct until Shep (dog) found one 23. Coyotes, owls, eagles, badgers eat ferrets 24. Climate is changing prairie into desert 25. Ferret survival tied to prairie dog	**~~Humans~~ Rancher Influence ~~Human Influence~~** Ranchers think prairie dog holes hurt cows Cows don't break legs in prairie dog holes Ranchers "plink" prairie dogs Ranchers have killed most prairie dogs **~~Ferrets~~ Ferret Facts** Ferrets are endangered Ferrets have a genetic bottleneck Reintroducing ferrets has been hard There are 3-4 kits in a ferret litter Limited DNA has made ferrets fragile Ferrets are bred in captivity and released Ferrets can get canine distemper Ferrets were thought extinct until Shep (dog) found one Coyotes, owls, eagles, badgers eat ferrets **Prairie Dogs** Prairie dogs are almost wiped out Prairie dogs are a keystone species Prairie dogs need (x) acres to live Prairie dogs, ferrets can get plague **Sharing Land ~~Animal Territories~~** Ferrets live in prairie dog holes Cows don't break legs in prairie dog holes Prairie dog digging helps natural prairie grasses grow Cows and bison like to eat near prairie dog burrows	**~~Environment~~ Environmental Threat** Cheatgrass is invading prairie Cheatgrass increases brush fire hazard Climate is changing prairie into desert Prairie is overgrazed **~~Ferrets and Prairie Dogs~~ Prairie Dog Importance** Ferrets live in prairie dog burrows A ferret eats 100 prairie dogs/year Ferret diet is 90% prairie dog Ferret survival tied to prairie dog **Ferret Threats** Cheatgrass increases brush fire hazard Ranchers "plink" prairie dogs Ferrets can get canine distemper Ferrets have genetic bottleneck Coyotes, owls, eagles, badgers eat ferrets **Recovery Challenges** Ferrets are endangered Ferrets have a genetic bottleneck There are 3-4 kits in a litter Prairie dogs are almost wiped out Ferret recovery has been expensive **~~Outside~~ Indirect Changes** Cheatgrass is invading prairie Climate is changing prairie into desert Ranchers "plink" (shoot) prairie dogs for sport Prairie dogs are almost wiped out	*Animal System* Prairie Dogs Prairie Dog Importance *Ferret Facts* Ferret Threats Recovery Challenges *Indirect Threats* Environmental Threat Rancher Influence ***Regroup***

STEP 4: REGROUP — 20-25 MINUTES

At the beginning of grouping and labeling, Ms. Marshall told the tables of students to create five groups with four items each. By the time they reported out all the original groups, there were nine groups on the board—all of which will be off limits as the tables begin regrouping. This increases the challenge, but it also sets the stage for more original, abstract thinking. As she gives verbal instructions Ms. Marshall walks around the room handing out task cards. Like Mr. Todd, Ms. Marshall is upbeat and energetic when she introduces this step; also like Mr. Todd, she adjusts the level of challenge by instructing her students to create only three new groups. Students work at their respective tables, searching for new ideas.

> ***Regrouping Task Card:***
> You've all done a GREAT job so far; now it's time to STRETCH! Using the items from our original list, create at least three completely new groups that help bring insight to our topic. The groups can have any number of items, but you can't use any item twice.
>
> - Create at least **three groups**
> - Each item should be used *only once*!
> - Keep your thinking loose! Believe it or not, it really helps to cluster your facts into groups first; then think about labels.
> - *After* you've created your groups, decide on a label.
>
> You have **FIVE MINUTES** to finish this task!

When they are done presenting their ideas, several unique, new groups are on the board. Ms. Marshall notices that the labels are much more abstract. There is no mention of prairie dogs, ranchers, ferrets or grass; instead, the labels focus on mistaken impressions, Interacting threats, and ways to go extinct. The tongue-in-cheek *Good Dog*! seems to be an exception. Ms. Marshall asks some probing questions in order to learn the intention underlying the label.

Ms. Marshall: *What do you mean by* Good Dog?

Rachel: *Like, the prairie dog is good for the ferret and good for the land and good for cows—it's a good dog!*

Ms. Marshall: *How is that different from this group we already have:* Prairie Dog Importance?

Leon: Prairie Dog Importance *is only about how they're important to ferrets. This is bigger, like, everything.*

Ms. Marshall: *What's the word for a plant or animal that is central to an ecosystem?*

Leon: *Keystone.*

Ms. Marshall: *So then, what's another name for the* Good Dog*?*

Rachel: Keystone Dog, *I guess, but I like* Good Dog *because it's the same idea but more fun.*

In the conversation above, Leon makes a distinction between the narrow boundary of *Prairie Dog Importance* and the broader scope of *Good Dog*. The students obviously understand the importance of the prairie dog as a keystone species, so Ms. Marshall accepts the argument that the creative label should stay in place.

STEP 5: GENERALIZE 15 MINUTES

All along, Ms. Marshall knew she would want to really focus on the final step of the lesson because her primary goal is to have her students grasp the importance of the concept systems. She asks the class to take a minute to review the ideas they've discussed. Then she asks her final focusing question:

Ms. Marshall: *Thinking about our entire conversation, including the list, all our groups and labels, and the hierarchy we created by subsuming groups, what general statements can we make about the prairie ecosystem?*

She instructs her students to discuss this question at their tables for a few minutes before they share ideas as a class. The students are surprised—they've been talking about ferrets, so a question about the prairie ecosystem seems like a bit of a leap. But they talk at their tables for a few minutes and finally offer some suggestions:

Human attitudes affect the prairie ecosystems.

The prairie ecosystem is like dominos, and the prairie dog is the first domino.

The prairie ecosystem is being hurt in obvious and not-so-obvious ways.

Ms. Marshall asks a few questions about each statement, ensuring that her students can make links back to the conversation.

- *In a system, what's another term for the domino effect?*
- *Let's work on the terms "obvious" and "not-so-obvious." If the "obvious" are direct effects, what are the "not-so-obvious"?*
- *What would you call human attitudes using systems terminology?*

As students answer her questions, the generalizations become even more abstract:

> *Negative inputs throw a system off balance.*
>
> *The prairie ecosystem has interactions throwing it off balance.*
>
> *The prairie ecosystem is being hurt in direct and indirect ways.*

The lesson is over, but Ms. Marshall wants to make sure that her students all understand the ideas they've discussed, so for homework, she tells the students to defend or amend one of the generalizations in a brief paragraph using at least three pieces of evidence to support their thinking.

SUMMARY: CONCEPT DEVELOPMENT WITH SMALL GROUPS

As predicted on Ms. Marshall's Cognitive Map, the students went from facts about ferrets to broad-based statements about what happens when one part of a system goes awry, all in the course of a single lesson. The path they took may not have been identical to Ms. Marshall's Cognitive Map, but it took the same direction and reached the same conclusions.

Small-group work is easy to incorporate into a Concept Development lesson; it helps vary the classroom environment, and it is perfect for block schedules. Better yet, students have fun working together and sharing their ideas. The following reminders will help ensure success when working with this more flexible form of the Concept Development model:

- Even when incorporating group work, the list should be created by the entire class.
- The middle steps, grouping and labeling, subsuming, and regrouping, are most conducive to small-group work.
- When using small groups, there will be more groups in the initial grouping and labeling step.
- When tables of students report the first sets of groups, items will already be cross-categorized.
- More opportunities to create hierarchies emerge during subsuming as a result of having more groups.
- Regrouping can be more challenging because more groups are put off limits. Students may need more moral support and, occasionally, helpful questions that suggest an initial direction.

CLASS RECORD OF CONCEPT DEVELOPMENT LESSON ON BLACK-FOOTED FERRET AND ECOSYSTEMS WITH REGROUPING

List	*Group and Label*		*Subsume* / *Regroup*

1. Ranchers think prairie dog holes hurt cows
2. Cheatgrass is invading prairie
3. Ferrets live in prairie dog holes
4. Ferrets are endangered
5. A ferret eats 100 prairie dogs/year
6. Prairie dogs are almost wiped out
7. Prairie dogs, ferrets can get plague
8. Ferret diet is 95% prairie dog
9. Ferrets have a genetic bottleneck
10. Cows don't break legs in prairie dog holes
11. Reintroducing ferrets has been hard
12. Prairie dogs are a keystone species
13. There are 3-4 kits in a ferret litter
14. Prairie dog digging helps natural prairie grasses grow
15. Cheatgrass increases brush fire hazard
16. Ranchers "plink" (shoot) prairie dogs for sport
17. Cows and bison like to eat near prairie dog burrows
18. Limited DNA has made ferrets fragile
19. Ferrets are bred in captivity and released
20. Ranchers killed most prairie dogs
21. Ferrets can get canine distemper
22. Ferrets were thought extinct until Shep (dog) found one
23. Coyotes, owls, eagles, badgers eat ferrets
24. Climate is changing prairie into desert
25. Ferret survival tied to prairie dog
	~~Humans~~ Rancher Influence ~~Human Influence~~
	Ranchers think prairie dog holes hurt cows
	Cows don't break legs in prairie dog holes
	Ranchers "plink" prairie dogs
	Ranchers have killed most prairie dogs
	
	~~Ferrets~~ Ferret Facts
	Ferrets are endangered
	Ferrets have a genetic bottleneck
	Reintroducing ferrets has been hard
	There are 3-4 kits in a ferret litter
	Limited DNA has made ferrets fragile
	Ferrets are bred in captivity and re-leased
	Ferrets can get canine distemper
	Ferrets were thought extinct until Shep (dog) found one
	Coyotes, owls, eagles, badgers eat fer-rets
	
	Prairie Dogs
	Prairie dogs are almost wiped out
	Prairie dogs are a keystone species
	Prairie dogs need (x) acres to live
	Prairie dogs, ferrets can get plague
	
	Sharing Land ~~Animal Territories~~
	Ferrets live in prairie dog holes
	Cows don't break legs in prairie dog holes
	Prairie dog digging helps natural prai-rie grasses grow
	Cows and bison like to eat near prairie dog burrows
		~~Environment~~ Environmental Threat
		Cheatgrass is invading prairie
		Cheatgrass increases brush fire hazard
		Climate is changing prairie into desert
		Prairie is overgrazed
		
		~~Ferrets and Prairie Dogs~~ Prairie Dog Importance
		Ferrets live in prairie dog burrows
		A ferret eats 100 prairie dogs/year
		Ferret diet is 90% prairie dog
		Ferret survival tied to prairie dog
		
		Ferret Threats
		Cheatgrass increases brush fire hazard
		Ranchers "plink" prairie dogs
		Ferrets can get canine distemper
		Ferrets have genetic bottleneck
		Coyotes, owls, eagles, badgers eat fer-rets
		
		Recovery Challenges
		Ferrets are endangered
		Ferrets have a genetic bottleneck
		There are 3-4 kits in a litter
		Prairie dogs are almost wiped out
		Ferret recovery has been expensive
		
		~~Outside~~ Indirect Changes
		Cheatgrass is invading prairie
		Climate is changing prairie into desert
		Ranchers "plink" (shoot) prairie dogs for sport
		Prairie dogs are almost wiped out
			Animal System
			  Prairie Dogs
			    Prairie Dog Importance
			
			Ferret Facts
			  Ferret Threats
			
			Recovery Challenges
			  Indirect Threats
			    Environmental Threat
			    Rancher Influence
			
			Regroup
			
			Mistaken Impressions
			Cows don't break legs in prairie dog holes
			Prairie dog digging helps natural prairie grasses grow
			Cows and bison like to eat near prairie dog burrows
			
			Interacting Threats
			Ferret is endangered
			Prairie dogs are almost wiped out
			Ferret tied to survival of prairie dog
			
			~~Ways to Go Extinct~~ Fatal Threats
			Ferret survival is tied to prairie dog
			Prairie dog is almost wiped out
			Cheatgrass increases brushfire hazard
			Prairie dogs, ferrets can get plague
			
			Good Dog!
			Prairie dogs are a keystone species
			Prairie dog digging helps natural prairie grasses grow
			Cows don't break legs in prairie dog holes
			Ferret diet is 95% prairie dog

Generalizations: *Negative inputs throw a system off balance. The prairie ecosystem has interactions throwing it off balance. The prairie system is being hurt in direct and indirect ways.*

Ms. Bryant teaches American History. She has struggled to find ways to get her students engaged in understanding the Constitutional Amendments—now she is going to give Concept Development a try. Like many high school teachers, she faces some constraints that seem to work against using a strategy like Concept Development. The first is the daily schedule: her school is on an alternating schedule in which she has students for 25 minutes one day and 75 minutes the next. The second constraint is time. Ms. Bryant has a tight pacing guide to follow, so she is interested in saving time without sacrificing high-quality thinking. She has figured out a way to spread the lesson over three days, using a homework assignment as a bridge.

PREPARING FOR THE LESSON

This lesson has a ready-made list: the Constitutional Amendments, including the Bill of Rights. As part of her preparation, Ms. Bryant creates a PowerPoint slide with the four-column chart, and she then writes each of the Amendments in a textbox. Using this set-up, she will be able to project the list onto her Smartboard and use her cursor to shift items around as the students create their groups. Ms. Bryant plans her lesson using a Cognitive Map (pp. 59-60). The process of thinking through the lesson helps her determine how much she will accomplish during the first 25-minute period and how she could use homework as a bridge between each day. While she sometimes uses Concept Development with small groups, for this lesson, she will work with the entire class.

STEP 1: LIST — 5 MINUTES

Like many secondary teachers, Ms. Bryant feels pressured for time, so she's glad that the list is already defined. Since the list is a given, the class moves directly into grouping and labeling.

Lesson Plan: *Concept Development*
Grade Level: *Secondary*
Purpose of Discussion: *To clarify and extend students' understanding of the Constitutional Amendments*
Background Information for Lesson: *Constitutional Amendments*

Concept Development	*Focusing Questions*	*Materials and Supports*
Step 1: List	*(Not necessary; list is given.)*	• List Amendments in movable boxes to project on Smartboard.
Step 2: Group and Label	<u>Grouping:</u> *Which of the Amendments share significant attributes (ideas) in common?* <u>Labeling:</u> *What are some possible labels for this cluster of Amendments? Which label seems to best capture the idea behind this group?*	• Give students think-pair-share-time before discussing possible groups. • Remember to ask for multiple ideas. • Ask for justification.
Step 3: Subsume	Homework: *Create a hierarchy of ideas based on the groups and labels we've created today.* Quick Summary Question (time permitting): *Based on our list, groups, and hierarchy, what insights are you gaining about the Constitution?*	• Change marker colors. • Report round-robin style again.
Step 4: Regroup and Label	*Find three brand new ways to group the Amendments. You can group any way you want as long as the group is <u>new</u> and <u>relevant</u> to our study of the Constitution.* Probe: *Which Amendments have not been used? Why do you suppose (x) doesn't group with the others?* *Which Amendments seem to be a reaction to a specific event?*	• Change marker colors. • Provide time to think beforehand.
Step 5: Generalize	*Thinking about our entire conversation, including the list, all of our groups and labels, and the hierarchy we created by subsuming groups, what general statements can we make about the rules that govern our country?*	• Give students a minute of individual think time to write down ideas before discussing as a class. • Start with one generalization, and have students integrate their ideas into the first.

Lesson Plan: *Concept Development*
Cognitive Map: *Constitutional Amendments*

Possible List	*Possible Groups and Labels*	*Possible Subsuming*	*Possible Regroups and Labels*
1. Freedom of Religion, Press, Expression 2. Right to Bear Arms 3. Quartering of Soldiers 4. Search and Seizure 5. Trial and Punishment, Compensation for Takings 6. Right to Speedy Trial, Confrontation of Witnesses 7. Trial by Jury in Civil Cases 8. Cruel and Unusual Punishment 9. Construction of Constitution 10. Powers of the States and People 11. Judicial Limits 12. Choosing the President, Vice President 13. Slavery Abolished 14. Citizenship Rights 15. Race No Barrier to Vote 16. Status of Income Tax Clarified 17. Senators Elected by Popular Vote 18. Liquor Abolished 19. Women's Suffrage 20. Presidential, Congressional Terms 21. Prohibition (Amend. 18) Repealed 22. Presidential Term Limits 23. Presidential Vote for District of Columbia 24. Poll Tax Barred 25. Presidential Disability and Succession 26. Voting Age Set to 18 Years 27. Limiting Changes to Congressional Pay	Arresting Citizens Quartering of Soldiers (3) Search and Seizure (4) Trial and Punishment (5) Cruel and Unusual (8) Citizen Equality Slavery Abolished (13) Citizenship Rights (14) Race No Barrier to Vote (15) Poll Tax Barred (24) Basic Rights Freedom of Religion, Press, Expression (1) Right to Bear Arms (2) Right to Speedy Trial (6) Trial by Jury in Civil Cases (7) Citizenship Rights (14) Electing Representatives Presidential, Congressional Terms (20) Presidential Term Limits (22) Choosing the President, Vice President (12) Senators Elected by Popular Vote (17) Added Rights Prohibition (Amend. 18) Repealed (21) Women's Suffrage (19) Voting Age Set to 18 (26) Presidential Vote for District of Columbia (23)	Basic Rights Arresting Citizens Electing Reps Citizen Equality	Undoing Mistakes Slavery Abolished (13) Prohibition (Amend. 18) Repealed (21) Poll Tax Barred (24) Presidents Choosing the President, Vice President (12) Presidential, Congressional Terms (20) Presidential Term Limits (22) Presidential Disability and Succession (25)

***Possible Generalizations:** The Constitution establishes citizen rights and protections. Government rights and protections change over time. In the U.S., rights have expanded over time.*

STEP 2: GROUP AND LABEL 20-25 MINUTES

Even though the list has already been decided, Ms. Bryant gives her students a minute to think-pair-share before launching into discussion. She knows her impulse was correct when she sees a few students opening the book to refresh their memories! They move through the first set of groups fairly quickly. Ms. Bryant focuses her questions on revealing additional insights about the first set of groups.

Ms. Bryant:	*I see that you have groups called* Aggression Protection *and* Fair Trial. *What do you notice about where these Amendments fall on the list?*
Trevor:	*They're the first ones.*
Ms. Bryant:	*What is the first set of Amendments called?*
Matt:	*The Bill of Rights.*
Ms. Bryant:	*Why do you suppose warfare and trial are so prominent in The Bill of Rights?*
Christina:	*Because these were the things we were really fighting the British about. They were the most important things at that time.*
Ms. Bryant.	*These Amendments address the burning issues of the day. What other group, if any, has Amendments that are clustered according to time as well as topic?*

This turns the students' attention to the group labeled *Slavery.*

Ms. Bryant:	*Someone remind me why we called this group* Slavery*?*
Jordan:	*Because they all deal with freeing the slaves.*
Ms. Bryant:	*Let's look at this more closely. How many of these deal with freeing the slaves?*
Christina:	*Those three that came all together: 13, 14, and 15. Not the one that barred the Poll Tax.*
Kate:	*Why not?*
Ms. Bryant:	*Someone help us understand why the Poll Tax does or doesn't fit under the label* Slavery.
Logan:	*Well, it has to do with race but not slaves since they were already freed when the Amendment was passed. I think the group should*

be called Freedom.

Kate: *Or* Racial Equality?

Ms. Bryant *Okay, class, which seems more appropriate for this group:* Race *or* Racial Equality?

Class: Racial Equality.

Ms. Bryant: *Liz, why do you think the label should be* Racial Equality?

Liz: *It says more; it's clearer than the others.*

Ms. Bryant changes the label on the board.

Ms. Bryant also sees that the group *Aggression Protection* only contains three items instead of four. Technically, it doesn't meet the guidelines she gave the students for grouping. However, it is an important category. She asks the students to go through the list again to make sure there are no other Amendments that will fit in that group and follows by asking them why they think there haven't been any other war-related Amendments. Ultimately, she leaves the group on the board. After all, the learning value of having this group on the board is much more important than holding to an arbitrary rule about grouping!

The 25 minutes have flown by, and class is over. Ms. Bryant ends this part of the lesson by assigning subsuming for homework. Each student is to create hierarchies using the groups and labels they just developed, along with a brief justification. She also reminds them that the assignment will be turned in for a grade.

STEP 3: SUBSUME 10-15 MINUTES

When the students arrive in class the next day, they see a warm-up activity on the board directing them to find two classmates and compare their hierarchies. When everyone is settled, Ms. Bryant has the class compare some of their hierarchies, and they quickly discuss some similarities and differences.

STEP 4: REGROUP 20-25 MINUTES

Ms. Bryant's classes are familiar with Concept Development, so they know what's coming next. In fact, during their last Concept Development lesson—on the events leading to Columbus's trip to the Americas—her students tried to finesse the challenge of regrouping by creating groups of items that all started with *s*: *Spain, Seeking, Sea,* and *Santa Maria!*

TWO STEPS OF CONCEPT DEVELOPMENT WITH CONSTITUTIONAL AMENDMENTS

List	*Group and Label*	*Subsume*	*Regroup*
1. Freedom of Religion, Press, Expression 2. Right to Bear Arms 3. Quartering of Soldiers 4. Search and Seizure 5. Trial and Punishment, Compensation for Takings 6. Right to Speedy Trial, Confrontation of Witnesses 7. Trial by Jury in Civil Cases 8. Cruel and Unusual Punishment 9. Construction of Constitution 10. Powers of the States and People 11. Judicial Limits 12. Choosing the President, Vice President 13. Slavery Abolished 14. Citizenship Rights 15. Race No Barrier to Vote 16. Status of Income Tax Clarified 17. Senators Elected by Popular Vote 18. Liquor Abolished 19. Women's Suffrage 20. Presidential, Congressional Terms 21. Prohibition (Amend. 18) Repealed 22. Presidential Term Limits 23. Presidential Vote for District of Columbia 24. Poll Tax Barred 25. Presidential Disability and Succession 26. Voting Age Set to 18 Years 27. Limiting Changes to Congressional Pay	Aggression Protection Right to Bear Arms (2) Quartering of Soldiers (3) Search and Seizure (4) Fair Trial Trial and Punishment (5) Speedy Trial (6) Trial by Jury (7) Cruel and Unusual Punishment (8) Judicial Limits (11) ~~Slavery~~ ~~Freedom~~ Racial Equality Slavery Abolished (13) Citizenship Rights (14) Race No Barrier to Vote (15) Poll Tax Barred (24) Election Rules Presidential, Congressional Terms (20) Presidential Term Limits (22) Choosing the President, Vice President (12) Senators Elected by Popular Vote (17) Expanded Rights Prohibition (Amend. 18) Repealed (21) Women's Suffrage (19) Voting Age Set to 18 (26) Presidential Vote for District of Columbia (23)		
Generalizations:			

Even though Ms. Bryant loves her feisty teenaged class, she closes the door to this avoidance strategy by carefully phrasing the focusing question:

> *Ms. Bryant:* *Now, find three brand new ways to group the Amendments. You can group any way you want as long as the group is new and relevant to our study of the Constitution.*

Once again, she gives them think-pair-share time to let them test their initial ideas before she engages the entire class in discussion. After working through a couple of unsuccessful combinations, they settle on three groups, shown in the table on page 66. As Ms. Bryant expected, there were some interesting opportunities for discussion. Some of her probing questions relate directly to the new groups, some to the trends she sees emerging.

> *What is the difference between the group* Election Rules *and the group* Voting Access*?*

> *Why is the second set of groups less chronological? What does that say about the issues important enough to amend the Constitution?*

> *Which, if any, of the Amendments is so unique that it does not group well? What about that Amendment makes it stand out?*

Ms. Bryant doesn't want to spend more than 30 minutes on the lesson today, as she is feeling the need to keep moving forward. Once again, she uses homework as a means of extending the Concept Development lesson, telling students to write draft generalizations responding to the following prompt:

> *Based on our conversation, all of the groups you've defined, the relationships between the groups, and even the Amendments that seem to stand alone, what are some general statements we can make about the role the Constitution plays in shaping our democracy?*

STEP 5: GENERALIZE 15 MINUTES

The following day, students once again find a warm-up activity related to the lesson. They are to select three or four classmates and compare generalizations, then refine the one they think best captures important ideas from their conversations. The ideas are put up on the Smartboard screen and saved.

The Constitution establishes citizen rights and protections.

Government rights and protections change over time.

In the U.S., rights have expanded over time.

Ms. Bryant takes the conversation one step further. She asks the students to look at the Concept Development chart and find four words that describe the central functions of the U.S. Constitution. The students select:

Rules
Rights
Freedoms
Limits

These words can serve as a thematic core for conversations about U.S. History for the rest of the school year.

SUMMARY: CONCEPT DEVELOPMENT OVER SEVERAL DAYS

Teachers across grade levels feel increasing pressure to focus on content coverage. This makes using critical thinking techniques seem like a luxury they can't afford. However, techniques like Concept Development, when judiciously used, can help students appreciate pivotal pieces of information, allowing them to become a point of reference for the rest of a unit, or even the rest of the year.

Concept Development loses value if steps are skipped or if the highest levels are left off the end. However, time savings are possible if initial work is completed as homework. This also allows a Concept Development lesson to be divided over several days. Some teachers find the idea of spending 20 minutes over three days easier to justify than spending an hour on a single day.

When dividing a Concept Development lesson over several days, follow these guidelines:

- Students can be assigned homework ahead of the lesson to bring 3-4 items for the list, but the list should be constructed as a class.

- Similarly, students can prepare for grouping and labeling or regrouping for homework, but these steps require discussion, so they can't be completed in their entirety as homework

- Subsuming and generalizing lend themselves to homework assignments; they are easier to complete individually and can be recorded quickly on the board when the lesson resumes the next day.

- Avoid always using the same step as a homework bridge.

COMPLETED CONCEPT DEVELOPMENT LESSON USING CONSTITUTIONAL AMENDMENTS

List	*Group and Label*	*Subsume*	*Regroup*
1. Freedom of Religion, Press, Expression 2. Right to Bear Arms 3. Quartering of Soldiers 4. Search and Seizure 5. Trial and Punishment, Compensation for Takings 6. Right to Speedy Trial, Confrontation of Witnesses 7. Trial by Jury in Civil Cases 8. Cruel and Unusual Punishment 9. Construction of Constitution 10. Powers of the States and People 11. Judicial Limits 12. Choosing the President, Vice President 13. Slavery Abolished 14. Citizenship Rights 15. Race No Barrier to Vote 16. Status of Income Tax Clarified 17. Senators Elected by Popular Vote 18. Liquor Abolished 19. Women's Suffrage 20. Presidential, Congressional Terms 21. Prohibition (Amend. 18) Repealed 22. Presidential Term Limits 23. Presidential Vote for District of Columbia 24. Poll Tax Barred 25. Presidential Disability and Succession 26. Voting Age Set to 18 Years 27. Limiting Changes to Congressional Pay	Aggression Protection Right to Bear Arms (2) Quartering of Soldiers (3) Search and Seizure (4) Fair Trial Trial and Punishment (5) Speedy Trial (6) Trial by Jury (7) Cruel and Unusual Punishment (8) Judicial Limits (11) ~~Slavery~~ ~~Freedoms~~ Racial Equality Slavery Abolished (13) Citizenship Rights (14) Race No Barrier to Vote (15) Poll Tax Barred (24) Election Rules Presidential, Congressional Terms (20) Presidential Term Limits (22) Choosing the President, Vice President (12) Senators Elected by Popular Vote (17) Expanded Rights Prohibition (Amend. 18) Repealed (21) Women's Suffrage (19) Voting Age Set to 18 (26) Presidential Vote for District of Columbia (23)	Expanded Rights *Aggress. Protect.* *Fair Trial* *Racial Equality*	Human Freedoms Freedom of Religion, Press, Expression (1) Slavery Abolished (13) Women's Suffrage (19) Right to Bear Arms (2) Prohibition (Amend. 18) Repealed (21) Procedural Rules Construction of Constitution (9) Powers of the States and People (10) Presidential Term Limits (22) Presidential, Congressional Terms (20) Government Limits Judicial Limits (11) Liquor Abolished (18) Limiting Changes to Congressional Pay (27) Cruel and Unusual Punishment (8) Voting Access Race No Barrier to Vote (15) Presidential Vote for DC (23) Poll Tax Barred (24) Voting Age Set to 18 Years (26) Women's Suffrage (19)

Generalizations: *The Constitution establishes citizen rights and protections. Government rights and protections change over time. In the U.S., rights have expanded over time.*

CHAPTER 5: PLANNING A CONCEPT DEVELOPMENT LESSON

Obviously no one can determine ahead of time exactly what will take place during a discussion, but if a teacher has thought through what he wants to accomplish and outlined the [questions] he will use and the response he can anticipate, his discussions are far more likely to be productive and well worth the time and energy spent in planning. (Taba, Durkin, Fraenkel, & McNaughton, 1971)

THE COGNITIVE MAP

Planning a sequence of questions requires thinking all the way through a lesson in advance. The Cognitive Map is the tool Taba developed to help teachers anticipate the progression of questions and responses in a lesson from beginning to end. Like a blueprint, the Cognitive Map helps teachers see the general shape a discussion might take as students respond to focusing questions. Taba saw the Cognitive Map as a means to:

- Explore a topic, seeing how the progression of ideas builds on each other and anticipating the variety of ideas likely to emerge in a discussion
- Develop focusing questions directly related to the topic of study
- Test the logic of relationships teachers hope to develop during a lesson (Taba et al., 1971)

Completing a Cognitive Map is not difficult; it simply requires doing the thinking students will do during the lesson. To get a better sense of how the Cognitive Map helps the process of planning a Concept Development lesson, we will once again join fourth-grade teacher Mr. Todd. The unit on interdependence is over, and the year is moving on. Mr. Todd is in the middle of a unit on transportation. Students have been researching different forms of transportation around the world, and he wants to help them make some connections, so he's planning a new Concept Development lesson. He's learned that the Cognitive Map helps him see important relationships ahead of time, so he pulls out a blank form and starts the planning process.

COMPLETING A COGNITIVE MAP

Each of the Taba strategies has a slightly different Cognitive Map. The Cognitive Map for Concept Development is divided into the different steps of the lesson, with room at the top to record the purpose of the lesson, the grade level, and the source of information students will use to create their list.

Purpose of Discussion: *Provide a clear, concise description of the idea under investigation.*

What to Do on the Cognitive Map: State the concept or idea you want students to explore using the format: "To clarify and extend students' concept of (concept)."

Cognitive Map for Concept Development

Purpose of Discussion: *To extend and clarify students' understanding of a prairie ecosystem*

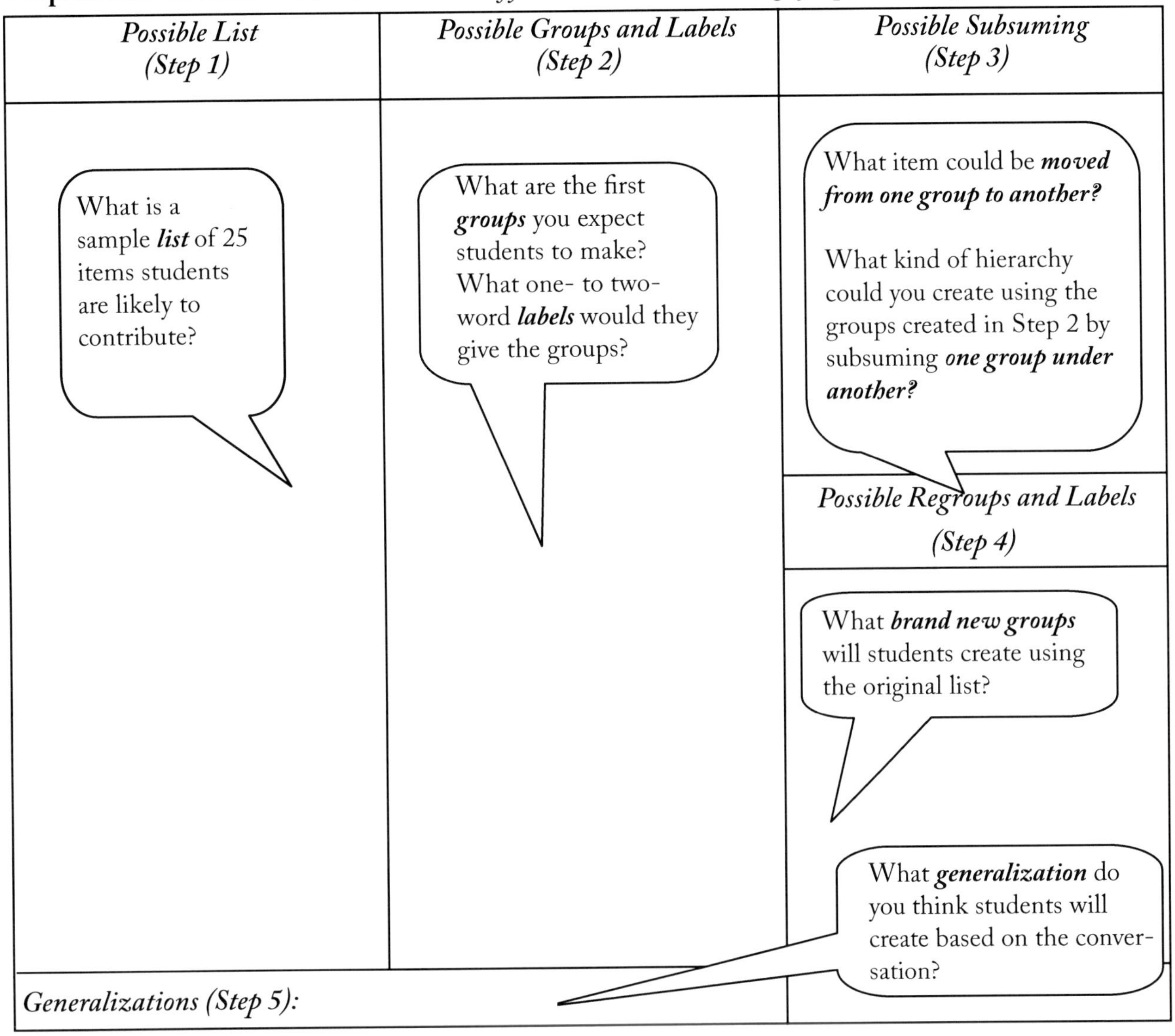

The purpose of any Concept Development lesson is for students to gain a deeper understanding of an idea or concept, so the first step when planning is to decide on the concept to explore. Make sure the concept or idea is clear enough to help establish a direction for the lesson. A lesson focused on animal *behaviors* will have a different result from a lesson on animal habitats; a lesson on animal *habitats* will be different from a lesson on animal *houses*. Several idea starters for Concept Development lessons in different subjects are included in Chapter 6.

The phrase "extend and clarify" is used as a reminder of the two overarching goals of Concept Development: 1) *extending* the breadth of students' understanding of concept, and 2) *clarifying* the meanings and relationships of ideas within the concept.

Mr. Todd has decided that he wants his students to explore the idea that people everywhere travel using transportation that matches different needs, so that is what he writes in the blank next to Purpose of Discussion: *To extend and clarify students' concept of variation in human transportation.*

Step 1: List

Create a sample list of about 25 items that lead to the purpose of discussion

What to Do on the Cognitive Map. Think of 25 items that will lead students to the topic entered as the purpose of discussion. Write these in the first column of the Cognitive Map.

Planning the list isn't difficult, but it's best to keep a few pointers in mind.

1. As your list evolves, think about the questions you might have to ask to prompt your students to volunteer these items (or similar items) during the actual lesson. No new items are added to the list after this step, so it's important that the 25 items on the board have the necessary variety .
2. The list should be long enough to present many options for grouping without becoming cumbersome or overwhelming. Students should have to use a majority of the items (for novice students) or all items (for experienced students), especially during the early grouping and labeling step.
3. Giving students a pre-made list makes sense when the content is already well-defined. However, giving the students a list does not save time. Students actually need more time to become familiar with the list if they don't create it themselves, and they lose the sense of ownership that is cultivated when they help the list take shape.
4. When working with younger students, it might be preferable to use pictures or objects as your "list." Toy zoo animals, pictures from nature, or common household tools could all become the focus of a Concept Development lesson.
5. Make sure the list is comprised of concrete or factual information. Avoid listing categories, as these can confuse the process of grouping and labeling later in the lesson and can ultimately make the regrouping step more difficult as well.

Mr. Todd's class has been researching transportation for two days, so he has little trouble creating a list with 25 different forms of transportation. Moreover, he's fairly confident that he can get his class to volunteer a fairly similar list, since students are bound to rely on the material they just read.

PARTIAL COGNITIVE MAP FOR CONCEPT DEVELOPMENT

Cognitive Map for Concept Development

Purpose of Discussion: *To extend and clarify students' concept of variation in human transportation*

Possible List (Step 1)	*Possible Groups and Labels (Step 2)*	*Possible Subsuming (Step 3)*
1. Car 2. Train 3. Airplane 4. Bus 5. Spaceship 6. Helicopter 7. Dog sled 8. Stagecoach 9. Horse 10. Bicycle 11. Motorcycle 12. Camel 13. Donkey 14. Rollerskates 15. Skateboard 16. Hang glider 17. Taxi 18. Subway/metro 19. Elephant 20. Canoe 21. Sailboat 22. Rickshaw 23. Skis 24. Chinese junk 25. Truck 26. Hot air balloon		 *Possible Regroups and Labels (Step 4)*
Possible Generalizations (Step 5):		

Step 2: Group and Label

Anticipate groups and labels students will create.

What to Do on the Cognitive Map. Create groups and labels just as you expect your students to do during the lesson, and write them in the second column of the Cognitive Map.

Step into the students' perspective, and anticipate the groups they are likely to create, as well as the hurdles they might experience. Use the same requirements for the number of groups and number of items in each group that you intend to give the students. Consider whether there is one step you want to emphasize over others in this lesson. Make notes about places where it might be helpful to pause and help students refine their thinking about an idea.

Mr. Todd proceeds with his Concept Map, working through the Concept Development strategy just as he hopes his students will. He follows the rules he expects to give the students: Find five groups, and put at least four items in each group. After working with the items for a while, he realizes that he can actually create six groups that use all of the items. Even if he doesn't require his students to meet this standard during the actual lesson, he's glad to have that option! He's also beginning to plan some questions about groups that might develop, for instance, about the necessity of having ways to travel without roads or about the many ways people find to travel together.

PARTIAL COGNITIVE MAP FOR CONCEPT DEVELOPMENT

Cognitive Map for Concept Development

Purpose of Discussion: *To extend and clarify students' concept of variation in human transportation*

Possible List (Step 1)	*Possible Groups and Labels (Step 2)*		*Possible Subsuming (Step 3)*
1. Car	Riding Animals	Road	
2. Train	Camel	Taxi	
3. Airplane	Donkey	Bus	
4. Bus	Elephant	Train	
5. Spaceship	Horse	Car	
6. Helicopter		Motorcycle	
7. Dog sled	Individual		
8. Stagecoach	Bicycle	Water-Based	
9. Horse	Skateboard	Sailboat	
10. Bicycle	Rollerskates	Chinese junk	
11. Motorcycle	Skis	Canoe	
12. Camel		Dog sled	
13. Donkey	Air-Based		
14. Rollerskates	Airplane	No Road	
15. Skateboard	Spaceship	Rickshaw	*Possible Regroups and Labels (Step 4)*
16. Hang glider	Hang glider	Stagecoach	
17. Taxi	Helicopter	Subway/metro	
18. Subway/metro	Hot air balloon	Train	
19. Elephant		Skis	
20. Canoe			
21. Sailboat			
22. Rickshaw			
23. Skis			
24. Chinese junk			
25. Truck			
26. Hot air balloon			
Possible Generalizations (Step 5):			

Step 3: Subsume

Find items that fit in different groups and/or groups that fit under the heading of other groups.

<u>What to Do on the Cognitive Map.</u> 1) Find items that could fit in more than one group. 2) Identify which groups could fit, in their entirety, under a different group. Write these in the third column of the Cognitive Map.

Continue to work from the students' perspective, finding items and groups to subsume. Consider the justifications students might provide for their suggestions, holding a conversation in your head to prepare your responses to their ideas. Spend some time predicting possible incorrect answers and how you might ask questions to help students see better choices.

Mr. Todd starts by considering which items in one group could also belong to a different group, even though his students are just about old enough to skip this part. Then he looks for a whole group that could be subsumed under another group. The groups sort themselves fairly naturally; however, he is interested to see that most of the forms of transportation actually don't use roads, something that might pique the students' curiosity when they realize that most of their personal transportation does require a road.

Step 4: Regroup

Create brand new groups using the original items.

<u>What to Do on the Cognitive Map.</u> Create several new groups using the items on the original list.

Planning for regrouping is very much like planning for grouping and labeling. The only exception is that groups created in the earlier step are put off limits. Students will not be allowed to recreate groups, nor will they be allowed to select the same items and give the group a different name. They are required to make entirely new groups and labels during this step.

Mr. Todd imagines what new groups his students might form if they can't use the groups *Riding Animals, Air-Based, Road, No Road, Individual,* or *Water-Based.* He finds that for this lesson, there are actually a fair number of new groups that don't require a significant "stretch." This makes him consider using small groups for this stage, since that will result in a wider range of ideas. Or he might require students to use the same number of items as they did in grouping and labeling, just to nudge the level of challenge up a notch.

Step 5: Generalize:

Create broad, general statements about the topic that are based on the class conversation.

<u>What to Do on the Cognitive Map:</u> Look over all of the groups and labels and the relationships that emerged during subsuming. Write some broad general statements

based on that information, avoiding statements that do not seem to be related to the information on the Cognitive Map.

A generalization is not difficult to write, but creating a generalization that connects back to the conversation requires a little more care. That is the goal of this step: not to create any generalization about humans and nature, but to ensure that students create generalizations that draw a connection between facts they've been discussing and abstract ideas. Consider the ideas you think students might suggest, and write them in the bottom section of the Cognitive Map.

Consistent with the strategy, Mr. Todd will have his students create generalizations to end the lesson. Sometimes he doesn't plan this step too closely—often his students' suggestions are better than the ones he makes anyway. Other times, he has a more certain sense of where he wants the lesson to end, and he wants to make sure his "target idea" emerges among the other ideas students will discuss. For this lesson, which follows a day of research, he would like for his students to gain a few insights about variation in transportation for individuals and groups. He writes some ideas in the Generalization section of the Cognitive Map, along with some other ideas he thinks the students might suggest.

COMPLETED COGNITIVE MAP FOR CONCEPT DEVELOPMENT

Cognitive Map for Concept Development

Purpose of Discussion: *To extend and clarify students' concept of variation in human transportation*

Possible List (Step 1)	*Possible Groups and Labels (Step 2)*		*Possible Subsuming (Step 3)*	
1. Car 2. Train 3. Airplane 4. Bus 5. Spaceship 6. Helicopter 7. Dog sled 8. Stagecoach 9. Horse 10. Bicycle 11. Motorcycle 12. Camel 13. Donkey 14. Rollerskates 15. Skateboard 16. Hang glider 17. Taxi 18. Subway/metro 19. Elephant 20. Canoe 21. Sailboat 22. Rickshaw 23. Skis 24. Chinese junk 25. Truck 26. Hot air balloon	Riding Animals Camel Donkey Elephant Horse Individual Bicycle Skateboard Rollerskates Skis Air-Based Airplane Spaceship Hang glider Helicopter Hot air balloon	Road Taxi Bus Train Car Motorcycle Truck Water-Based Sailboat Chinese junk Canoe Dog sled No Road Rickshaw Stagecoach Subway/metro Train Skis	Individual Riding Animals No Road Air-Based Water-Based (Riding Animals) Road	
			Possible Regroups and Labels (Step 4)	
			Many People Stagecoach Bus Airplane Train Subway/metro Entertainment Skateboard Hang glider Rollerskates Skis No Gasoline Sailboat Horse Skateboard Dog sled Bicycle	Old Forms Chinese junk Camel Stagecoach Canoe Motorized Taxi Spaceship Car Helicopter Trucks Exploration Spaceship Canoe Dog sled

Possible Generalizations (Step 5): *People invented large machines (like trains, planes, and boats) so many people can travel at the same time. Some transportation changes with region.*

WRITING FOCUSING QUESTIONS FOR THE LESSON PLAN

As he works on the Cognitive Map, Mr. Todd jots down notes about the focusing questions that he might need at each step of the lesson. Focusing questions introduce each step of the lesson or redirect the conversation if students stray off track. However, these are not the only questions Mr. Todd will ask. Sophistication in instructing Concept Development comes from blending focusing questions with probing questions that pursue students' reasoning.

The First Focusing Question

Starting the List

The first focusing question starts the process of generating the list. It's important that the question is focused so that students offer items that will ultimately lead to the purpose of discussion. Having completed his Cognitive Map, Mr. Todd has a good sense of the items he wants on the list: different types of transportation. However, he knows from experience that if he just walks in the classroom and throws out a question like:

How do people get around?

he's likely to get a number of answers he doesn't really want, like walking, running, or hopping.

The question "How do people get around?" is too open and needs clearer focus. He tries a revision:

~~How do people get around?~~

What forms of transportation do we use?

Mr. Todd is barely finished writing the question when he realized that it was a bit too narrow—he and his students only use a few forms of transportation used in the world! He tries again:

~~What forms of transportation do we use?~~

What forms of transportation do people around the world use to go faster or farther than they can go on foot?

This question seems about right. It is open-ended but includes "clues" to direct students' thinking toward the specific kinds of transportation he wants them to work with during the lesson.

Remaining Focusing Questions

Grouping and Labeling, Subsuming, Regrouping, and Generalizing

The focusing questions that begin the remaining steps of Concept Development are fairly standard, prompting students to move to the next step. Mr. Todd often plans a broad question and a second question that is open-ended but more focused. These second questions are Mr. Todd's back-up plan just in case the students don't understand what he wants from the broader question. For instance, under subsuming, he has both a broad question:

> Which of the items under one group could also go in another group?

and a more specific question:

> I see that *Dog sled* is in the group *Water-Based.* Where else might *Dog sled* fit?

As Mr. Todd proceeds, he chooses his focusing questions and then considers the materials he will need to support instruction. Included among the supports are some familiar activities that help students generate ideas. For example, he plans to use a quick think-pair-share in preparation for grouping and labeling.

When he's finished, Mr. Todd has thought through the lesson from beginning to end. He has written focusing questions and listed activities and materials that will help the lesson move smoothly. More importantly, he has already talked through the conversation in his head. Even thought the conversation is bound to unfold somewhat differently, this "rehearsal" will help him keep his goals in sight.

SAMPLE FOCUSING QUESTIONS FOR CONCEPT DEVELOPMENT

Lesson Plan: *Concept Development*
Grade Level: *Elementary.*
Purpose of Discussion: *To extend and clarify students' concept of variation in human transportation*
Background Information for Lesson: *Personal experience*

Concept Development	*Focusing Questions*	*Materials and Supports*
Step 1: List	*What forms of transportation do people around the world use to go faster or farther than they can go on foot?*	• Provide pictures of various forms of transportation around the room. • Refer students to textbooks. • Allow students to talk to a partner for a minute before gathering the list.
Step 2: Group and Label Mr. Todd likes to include the word *important* because it deters grouping based on the first letter of the words or other trivial reasons.	Grouping: *Which items on our list can we group together based on an important shared characteristic? Why do these items go together?* or *Which items could go together because they are alike in an important way?* Labeling: *What one- to two-word label would best describe this group?*	• Provide guidelines: Students must create at least five groups and can have no more than five items left. • Give students time to think-pair-share before beginning class discussion. • Use the second column to record answers. • Change marker color. • List groups; then go back and label.
Step 3: Subsume	*Which of the items under one group could also go under another group?* or *I see that "sailboat" is under the group "Water-Based." Where else might "sailboat" fit? What makes you think that "sailboat" could belong in that group?*	• Change marker colors. • Show hierarchy by listing in outline form on the board.
Step 4: Regroup	*So far, so good! Now what completely new ways can you find to group the items on our list?* *If necessary: If you shift your thinking from where it transports you to how some are similar, what new groups do you see?*	• Change marker colors. • Provide time to think before discussion.
Step 5: Generalize	*Based on our original list, the groups we've created, and the way we subsumed the groups, what would you conclude about the types of transportation people use?*	• Give students a minute of individual think time to write down ideas before discussing as a class. • Gather a few ideas, and then select one or two as a class to incorporate other ideas into.

PRACTICE

Exercise 1A: This Cognitive Map contains a list of zoo animals. Work on your own or with colleagues to complete the rest of the Cognitive Map.

Cognitive Map for Concept Development

Purpose of Discussion: ______________________________

Possible List (Step 1)	*Possible Groups and Labels (Step 2)*	*Possible Subsuming (Step 3)*
1. Lion 2. Tiger 3. Polar bear 4. Grizzly bear 5. Koala bear 6. Kangaroo 7. Flamingo 8. Snake 9. Penguin 10. Otter 11. Anteater 12. Hippo 13. Giraffe 14. Zebra 15. Elephant 16. Seal 17. Cheetah 18. Deer 19. Parrot 20. Screech owl 21. Iguana 22. Tortoise 23. Crocodile 24. Toucan 25. Chimpanzee		 *Possible Regroups and Labels (Step 4)*

Possible Generalizations (Step 5):

Exercise 1B: What focusing question could you ask to prompt students to create a list like the one in Practice Exercise 1A?

____

____

What follow-up questions would you ask in order to make sure the list has the desired breadth?

____

____

What would you ask to ensure that students were listing specific examples instead of categories?

____

____

Exercise 2: What questions would you ask to create a broad-based 25-item list of:

Flowers?

____

____

Types of cars?

____

____

Songs?

____

____

Exercise 3: Two focusing questions are listed below. Create lists like the ones you imagine students would create in response to each question.

Question: *What are some items someone in your family bought in a store last week?*	Question: *What did someone in your family spend money on last week?*

Reflect: How are the lists different? How might the differences affect the direction of the lesson?

____

____

____

CHAPTER 6: LESSON STARTERS AND MODEL LESSON PLANS

A cognitive map…suggests some of the directions and the levels of ideas that responses in a discussion could take as pupils pursue a question. The map helps the teacher to anticipate the discussion because it demonstrates any number of acceptable answers to a question. As the teacher listens to the contributions of the pupils, he can anticipate whether a particular remark may lead the class discussion; he is able to distinguish a valid and promising leader from an irrelevant, unfruitful, or illogical one. (Taba, 1967, pp. 64)

Lists for a Concept Development lesson can come from almost anywhere. The focusing questions on the next page are just a small sample of possible ways to begin a Concept Development lesson.

The majority of this chapter is comprised of sample lesson plans to give a sense of what a Concept Development lesson plan might look like for different age groups and in different subject areas. The lessons also show different ways to prepare for the lesson, to vary instruction, and to phrase important questions.

An effort was made to show different ways to incorporate core content. For example, there is a mathematics lesson in which students use Cuisenaire rods on a table instead of working with words on a whiteboard. Two lessons give different treatments of the novel *To Kill a Mockingbird*, one using a list of characters and the other using a list of key events. Examples from science and social studies are also included.

FIRST FOCUSING QUESTIONS

What are some things people do when they…

prepare to pay taxes, get mad, build a deck, persuade someone, create a law, change group behavior, conduct an experiment

What comes to mind when you hear the word…

civilization, friendship, communism, mathematics, hero, villain, conflict

What do you know about (or what did you learn about)…

oceans, the reign of Henry VIII, the Roaring '20s, the solar system, economic trends, fractals, chemical reactions, the life of Frederick Douglass, growing plants, winter holidays, Nobel Laureates

What did you observe at/in…

our field trip, the movie, a painting, our neighborhood walk, a 100s chart

What are examples of…

services provided by the (federal, state, local) government, things people sell, reasons people came to America, what is needed to start a business, real-world use of mathematics

What are the parts of…

a democracy, being a family, a healthy meal, an effective essay, an engine, government, graphs, the solar system, poetry, mathematical formulas, electrical grids

What do you find in a...

newspaper, grocery store, city, forest, desert, hardware store, school, community, bank, library, nuclear power plant

What are some consequences of…

life changing events, changing variables in an experiment, changing seasons, clear-cutting forests, Westward expansion

What are ways…

people use fractions, to communicate, land is used, we use electricity, nature affects human behavior, to name the number 12, to measure, people earn a living

Lesson Plan: *Concept Development*
Grade Level: *Primary*
Purpose of Discussion: *To extend and clarify students' concept of word sounds*
To build students' skills in grouping
Background Information for Lesson: *(Given) short* i *list from a word wall*

Note: *This lesson, designed for early primary grades, is intended to teach about grouping as much as it is about short* i *words. The lesson is based on 25 items, but it would work as well with 15 words—just make sure to adjust the number of groups required, too. Try asking students to create five groups with three items each.*

Concept Development	***Focusing Questions***	***Materials and Supports***
Step 1: List	*Not necessary; list is given.* If desired: *What other short* i *words could we add to this list?*	• Have cards with one word each available to work with either as a group or at tables.
Step 2: Group and Label	Grouping: *Which of these words have something in common? Let's see if we can create groups with four words that are alike in some way. Why do you think these words go together?* Labeling: *What would be a good name to describe this group?*	• Provide rules for grouping: five groups with four items in each group. • Record answers in the second column of the chart. • Change marker colors so students can follow the progression of ideas.
Step 3: Subsume	*Which word that is in one group could also belong to another group?* If necessary: *What other word could also fit in (x) group? Why do you think it could be a member of both groups?*	• Use the third section of the chart. • Shift cards so students can find one word belonging to two different groups.
Step 4: Regroup	*You've done a great job so far! Let's set these groups aside and try to create three new groups using these words.*	• Provide a short timeline to increase on-task behavior. • Provide encouragement for students who are struggling to find new ideas. • Suggest that students find three new groups with three items each.
Step 5: Generalize	*Thinking about our entire conversation, including the list, all of our groups and labels, and the ways some words fit in more than one group, what are some things we can say about short* i *words? What can we say about the ways that words are put together?*	• Allow students a minute to think and share ideas with a partner before beginning discussion.

Cognitive Map for Concept Development

Purpose of Discussion: *To extend and clarify students' understanding of words with short* i *sounds*

Possible List (Step 1)	*Possible Groups and Labels (Step 2)*	*Possible Subsuming (Step 3)*
1. Fish 2. In 3. His 4. It 5. Lip 6. Wind 7. Sip 8. Is 9. Trip 10. Win 11. If 12. Sit 13. Dip 14. This 15. Dish 16. Miss 17. Lift 18. Hip 19. Fit 20. Him 21. Hit 22. Kit 23. Flip 24. Slim 25. Clip	<u>Two-letter words starting with i</u> In It Is If <u>*It* Words</u> It Sit Fit Kit Hit <u>*is* inside</u> Fish Miss His This Dish <u>Has *ip*</u> Lip Sip Trip Hip Flip Clip <u>Four letters</u> Wind Dish Miss Lift Clip Slim Fish Trip This Flip	<u>Four letters</u> Wind Dish Miss Lift Trip <u>is inside</u> <u>Has *ip*</u> Lip Sip Trip Hip Clip ***Possible Regroups and Labels (Step 4)*** <u>Movement Words</u> Wind Trip Lift Flip <u>3 Consonants</u> Trip This Flip Slim Fish Wind Dish Miss Lift Clip

Possible Generalizations (Step 5): *Short* i *sounds are at the beginning and middle of a word. Word sounds help rhyming happen because they end the same. Short* i *can be in words of different sizes.*

Cognitive Map format adapted from the Institute for Staff Development (1971).

Lesson Plan: *Concept Development*
Grade Level: *Primary*
Purpose of Discussion: *To extend and clarify students' concept of numbers and addition*
Background Information for Lesson: *(Given) Cuisenaire rod combinations*
Note: *This lesson is a variation of a lesson in the Taba for Concept Development from the Institute for Staff Development. The lesson uses a table divided into four sections instead of a chart on a wall or board so that primary-level students can work with Cuisenaire rods. Also notice that during subsuming, the teacher actually creates a higher-level grouping for the students to use.*

Because of the short list of data and the age group, the "five groups with four items" rule is not used in this lesson.

Concept Development	*Focusing Questions*	*Materials and Supports*
Step 1: List	*Not necessary; list is given.*	• Divide a work table into four sections.
Step 2: Group and Label	Grouping: *What groups can we make based on something the rows share in common?* *How are certain rows of blocks alike?* Labeling: *What name can we give to this group of rows? Why do you think that is a good label for this group?*	• Have additional rods available to rebuild rows in the groups and labels section of the table. • Ask for justification.
Step 3: Subsume	*Which of our groups could fit into a big group called* Red and White*?* *Which of our groups could fit into a bigger group called* Uses Green*?*	• Create groups of the hierarchies with new Cuisenaire rods/blocks in the third section of the table.
Step 4: Regroup	*What new groups can we create with these same rows?* *What can we look at besides the combination of colors in rows?* If necessary: *The rows might have the same colors or the same kind of patterns. There are lots of ways to look at these.* *For instance, how many rows have just one white block? How many of you think that could be a group?*	• Build new groups in the fourth section of the table. • If necessary, reorganize the rows to make it easier for students to see different relationships.
Step 5: Generalize	*Thinking about our entire conversation and all of the ways we put the different groups of five together, what can we say about ways to make the number 5?* *What can we say about how addition works?*	• Have chart paper near the table to write students' ideas on.

Cognitive Map for Concept Development

Cuisenaire Rods

Possible List (Step 1)

Possible Groups and Labels (Step 2)

2 Reds, 1 White

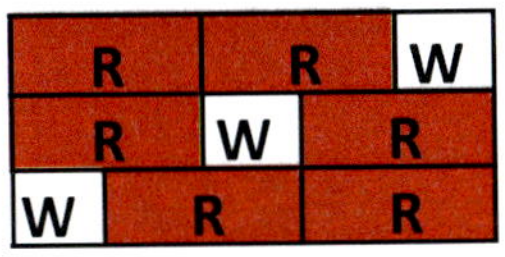

1 Green, 2 Whites

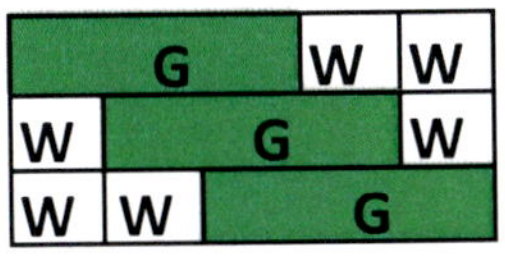

1 Purple, 1 White

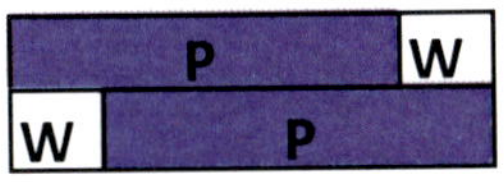

5 Whites

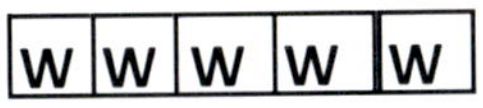

1 Red, 1 Green

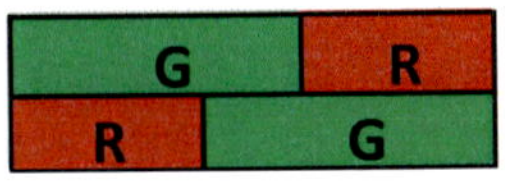

3 Whites, 1 Red

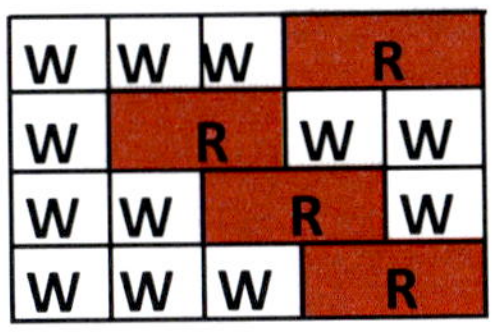

Possible Subsuming (Step 3)

White and Red

- 2 Reds, 1 White
- 3 Whites, 1 Red

Uses Green

- 1 Green, 2 Whites
- 1 Red, 1 Green

Possible Regroups and Labels (Step 4)

Rows with 1 White

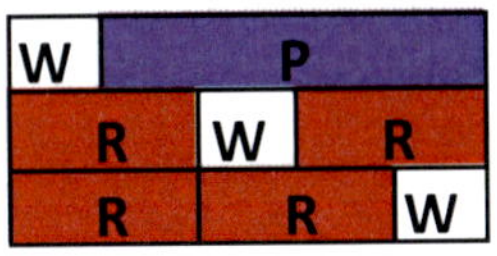

Rows with Rods Shorter than Green

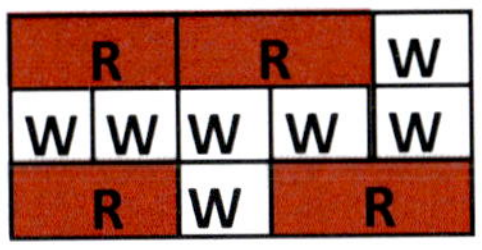

Rows with Two Pieces

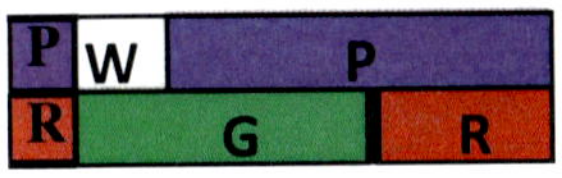

Possible Generalizations (Step 5): 5 is made of many combinations of 1, 2, 3, and 4. The order of the numbers does not matter when adding.

Cognitive Map format adapted from the Institute for Staff Development (1971).

Lesson Plan: *Concept Development*
Grade Level: *Elementary*
Purpose of Discussion: *To extend and clarify students' concept of communication*
Background Information for Lesson: *Personal experience, observation*

Concept Development	*Focusing Questions*	*Materials and Supports*
Step 1: List	*What are some ways people communicate without speaking?* *How do we get to send a message without using words?* *If you couldn't talk, what would you do to tell me how you felt or what you thought?*	• Give students time to write down a few ideas. • Have students act out non-verbal communication. • Have pictures of nonverbal communication posted around the room to generate ideas.
Step 2: Group and Label	<u>Grouping:</u> *Which of these go together because they are alike in some way?* *Why do you think (x) belongs in this group?* <u>Labeling:</u> *Thinking about the reasons why you put these together, what would be some good names for your groups?* *What name would you give this group?*	• Provide rules for grouping: five groups with four items in each group. • Record answers in the second column of the chart. • Ask students to support/explain their reasoning. • Change marker colors so students can follow the progression of ideas.
Step 3: Subsume	*What other group could (x) go in? Why?* *Where else might (y) fit? How is it that (y) could belong to both groups?* Summary Question: *Looking at these groups we've created, what are some ideas you are beginning to have about sending messages without words?*	• Use the third section of the chart. • Change marker colors. • Ask students to support/explain their reasoning.
Step 4: Regroup	*Let's put these first groups aside and find three brand new groups that show us something new about nonverbal communication.*	• Create one new group together to stimulate ideas; have students work in small groups to create the remainder of the new groups. • Suggest that students find three new groups with three items each. • Ask students to support/explain their reasoning. • Record ideas in the fourth column with a new color.
Step 5: Generalize	*Based on our discussion and looking at the different groups and labels, what are some general statements we can make about communicating without words, or nonverbal communication?*	• Have students work in groups to come up with ideas. Gather one idea per group before discussing the ideas. • Ensure that students can connect their generalization to the discussion.

Cognitive Map for Concept Development
Purpose of Discussion: To *extend and clarify students' understanding of nonverbal communication*

Possible List (Step 1)	*Possible Groups and Labels (Step 2)*	*Possible Subsuming (Step 3)*
1. Jump 2. Smile 3. Wave 4. Whistle 5. Clap 6. Groan 7. Tilt head 8. Stomp 9. Hit 10. Laugh 11. Point 12. Draw 13. Write 14. Act out 15. Wink 16. Thumbs down 17. Thumbs up 18. Shake finger 19. Roll eyes 20. Yawn 21. Look at watch 22. Tap foot 23. Drum fingers 24. Kick 25. Shrug shoulders	Noisy Yawn Drum fingers Laugh Whistle Clap Groan Tap foot Stomp Feet Jump Tap foot Stomp Kick Hands Shake finger Wave Thumbs up Thumbs down Drum fingers Arms and Hands Clap Point Shrug shoulders Draw Hit Write Face Smile Wink Roll eyes Tilt head	Noisy Yawn Drum fingers Laugh Whistle Clap Stomp Tap foot Arms and Hands Clap Point Shrug shoulders Draw Hands Face Smile Wink Roll eyes Tilt head Yawn Laugh Whistle *Possible Regroups and Labels (Step 4)* Good News Smile Laugh Clap Wink Dramatic Act out Roll eyes Groan Stomp Warning Tap foot Groan Point Look at watch
Possible Generalizations (Step 5): *People can communicate information and feelings without words. Non-verbal communication can be noisy or quiet. People can communicate using many parts of their body.*		

Cognitive Map format adapted from the Institute for Staff Development (1971).

Lesson Plan: *Concept Development*
Grade Level: *Elementary*
Purpose of Discussion: *To extend and clarify students' concept of rock formations*
Background Information for Lesson: *Chapter in science book, video on rocks*

Concept Development	*Focusing Questions*	*Materials and Supports*
Step 1: List	*Based on what you have learned in the book, the video, and your own experience, what facts do you know about rocks?* *What happens to rocks over time?* *What are signs of rocks aging?*	• Each student gathers 10 rock facts from their book and the video. • Make sure students give facts, not opinions. • Make sure the facts are about rocks, not uses for rocks.
Step 2: Group and Label	<u>Grouping:</u> *Looking at the list that we have, which items can be grouped together?* *What do these things have in common?* <u>Labeling:</u> *Thinking about why you grouped these items together, what are some possible names for this group?* *Why is that a good name for the group?*	• Provide rules for grouping: five groups with four items in each group. • Record answers in the second column of the chart. • Change marker colors so students can follow progression of ideas.
Step 3: Subsume	*What other groups could (x) fit under?* *Why would (x) fit into that group?* *Which entire group could we put under the heading of another group?* *Why would these labels apply to this group?* Summary Question: *Who would like to summarize what we know about rocks based on these groupings?*	• Use the third section of the chart. • Change marker colors so students can follow progression of ideas.
Step 4: Regrouping	*Looking at our list of data again, what entirely new groups could we make?*	• Provide encouragement for students who are struggling to find new ideas. • Suggest that students find three new groups with three items each.
Step 5: Generalize	*Based on the facts about rocks, the groups, and the labels we have created, what relationship do you see between physical structure, change, and time?* *What information did you use as the basis for our general statement?* *Which of these statements mean nearly the same thing? Which could go together?*	• Start with one or two statements, and have students add to them and adapt them to incorporate their ideas.

Cognitive Map for Concept Development
Purpose of Discussion: *To extend and clarify students' concept of rock formations.*

Possible List (Step 1)	*Possible Groups and Labels (Step 2)*	*Possible Subsuming (Step 3)*	*Possible Regroups and Labels (Step 4)*
1. Sedimentary 2. Igneous 3. Metamorphic 4. Color 5. Texture 6. Luster 7. Hardness 8. Minerals 9. Sand 10. Limestone 11. Sandstone 12. Granite 13. Rock cycle 14. Erosion 15. Weathering 16. Heat 17. Pressure 18. Layers 19. Lava 20. Fossils 21. Marble 22. Soil 23. Bedrock 24. Sediment 25. Melting	Rock Properties Color Texture Luster Hardness Rock Examples Limestone Sandstone Granite Marble Rock Parts Layers Fossils Sediments Minerals Earth Layers Soil Sand Bedrock Lava Change Rocks Erosion Weathering Heat Melting Pressure	Rock Parts Earth Layers Rock Examples Change Rocks Rock Properties	Surface Soil Sand Sandstone Deep Metamorphic Granite Lava Rock Morphing Limestone Pressure Heat Marble Valued Color Luster Marble
Possible Generalizations (Step 5): Time changes the physical placement of rocks. Time changes rocks' physical structure, some faster than others.			

Cognitive Map format adapted from the Institute for Staff Development (1971).

Lesson Plan: *Concept Development*
Grade Level: *Elementary*
Purpose of Discussion: *To extend and clarify students' concept of animal life/bats*
Background Information for Lesson: *Research on bats*

Concept Development	*Focusing Questions*	*Materials and Supports*
Step 1: List	*What did you learn about bats from your reading?* *What facts did you already know about bats?*	• Each student gathers 10 bat facts from their book. • Make sure students give facts, not opinions. • Make sure the facts offer enough variety
Step 2: Group and Label	Grouping: *Which of these words/phrases go together because they are alike in some way?* *Why do you think (x) belongs in this group?* Labeling: *Thinking about the reasons why you put these together, what would be some good names for your groups?* *What name would you give this group?*	• Provide rules for grouping: five groups with four items in each group. • Record answers in the second column of the chart. • Change marker colors so students can follow the progression of ideas.
Step 3: Subsume	*We put (x) in this group. What other groups could it go into?* *Which groups could fit inside another group?* *Why would you put (y) in that group?* *What entire group could we fit under or inside another entire group?* *Who would like to summarize what we know about bats based on these groupings?*	• Use the third section of the chart. • Make sure students provide reasons to support their ideas. • Allow students to create higher-level labels to subsume groups if necessary.
Step 4: Regroup	*What are some new categories for our information about bats?*	• Start this step with a five-minute time limit; extend as necessary. • Provide encouragement for students who are struggling to find new ideas. • Suggest that students find three new groups with three items each.
Step 5: Generalize	*Based on our discussion and looking at the different groups, what are some things we can say in general about bats in our world?* *What information did you use to come up with your statements?* *Which of these statements mean nearly the same thing?*	• Allow students a minute to think and share ideas with a partner before beginning discussion. • Post final generalizations on a bulletin board, and encourage students to bring articles in to post under the appropriate generalizations.

Cognitive Map for Concept Development

Purpose of Discussion: *To extend and clarify students' concept of animal life/bats*

Possible List (Step 1)	*Possible Groups and Labels (Step 2)*	*Possible Subsuming (Step 3)*	*Possible Regroups and Labels (Step 4)*
1. Light-weight bones 2. Echolocation 3. Nocturnal 4. Mammals 5. Eat fruit, insects, rodents 6. Drink blood 7. Almost 1000 species 8. Different sizes 9. Different diets 10. Live in trees 11. Live in buildings 12. Live in caves 13. Fly 14. Hand, including thumb 15. Get into attics 16. Pointy ears 17. Different colors 18. Make a screechy sound 19. Furry 20. Have live births 21. Some live 30 years 22. Some hibernate 23. Can get rabies 24. Help control insect population 25. Taught us about radar 26. Spread seeds	<u>Where They Live</u> Live in trees Live in buildings Live in caves Get into attics <u>Physical Description</u> Light-weight bones Hand, including thumb Pointy ears Make a screechy sound Furry <u>Variations</u> Different colors Different sizes Different diets Some hibernate Almost 1000 species <u>Help Humans</u> Taught us about radar Spread seeds Help control insect population Eats fruit, insects, rodents <u>Bat Behaviors</u> Fly Drink blood Have live births Nocturnal Echolocation	<u>Habits</u> Where They Live Help Humans <u>Physical Description</u> Variations	<u>How They Are Like Humans</u> Different sizes Live in buildings Hands, including thumbs Have live births <u>Scare Humans</u> Get into attics Drink blood Nocturnal Can get rabies
Possible Generalizations (Step 5): Human fear of bats can mask the benefits they bring. Even animals that seem very different have some similarities to humans.			

Lesson Plan: *Concept Development*
Grade Level: *Elementary*
Purpose of Discussion: *To extend and clarify students' concept of family wants and needs*
Background Information for Lesson: *Personal experience*

Concept Development	***Focusing Questions***	***Materials and Supports***
Step 1: List	*What are some things your family spent money on this week?*	• Give students time to write down a few ideas. • Gather data by getting one fact from each student.
Step 2: Group and Label	Grouping: *Which of these go together because they are alike in some way?* *Why do you think (x) belongs in this group?* Labeling: *Thinking about the reasons why you put these together, what would be some good names for your groups?*	• Provide rules for grouping: five groups with four items in each group. • Record answers in the second column of the chart. • Change marker colors so students can follow the progression of ideas.
Step 3: Subsume	*What other group could (x) go in? Why?* *Where else might (y) fit? How is it that (y) could belong to both groups?* Summary Question: *What are you beginning to notice about the ways families spend money?*	• Use the third section of the chart. • Change marker color. • Have specific examples ready from the Cognitive Map in order to ask open but directed questions to start the step: *Where else could we put (y)? What item could fit in both group (a) and group (b)?*
Step 4: Regroup and Label	*Let's put these first groups aside and find three others, brand new groups that show us something new about how families spend money.*	• Change marker color, and move to the fourth column. • Give a short time limit to increase on-task behavior. • Provide encouragement for students who are struggling to find new ideas. • Suggest that students find three new groups with three items each.
Step 5: Generalize	*Based on our discussion and looking at the different groups and labels, what are some general statements we can make about the way families spend money?* *What can we say about money and things families want and need?*	• Start with one or two statements and have students add to them and adapt it to incorporate their ideas. • Have students create a class tree map of the ideas discussed in this lesson.

Cognitive Map for Concept Development

Purpose of Discussion: *To extend and clarify students' understanding of family wants and needs*

<table>
<tr><th>Possible List (Step 1)</th><th>Possible Groups and Labels (Step 2)</th><th>Possible Subsuming (Step 3)</th></tr>
<tr>
<td rowspan="3">1. Shoes
2. Flowers
3. Pipe for the sink
4. Meat
5. Soup
6. Paint
7. Movie tickets
8. Popcorn
9. Shirt
10. Dog food
11. Repairman-refrigerator
12. Doctor-sick visit
13. Gasoline
14. Lawn service
15. Internet service
16. Cell phone
17. Oranges
18. Medicine
19. Magazines
20. Haircut
21. Flash drive
22. Monopoly game
23. Shaving cream
24. Teeth cleaning
25. Video rental
26. Piano lessons
27. Cable TV</td>
<td rowspan="3">People Food
Meat
Soup
Popcorn
Oranges

Relaxation
Movie tickets
Video rental
Monopoly game
Magazines
Piano lessons

Looking Good
Shoes
Shirt
Teeth cleaning
Haircut
Shaving cream

Home Care
Flowers
Lawn service
Cable TV
Paint
Repair refrig-erator</td>
<td>Home Care
Flowers
Lawn service
Cable TV
Paint
Repairman-refrigerator
Looking Good

Relaxation
People Food</td>
</tr>
<tr><th>Possible Regroups and Labels (Step 4)</th></tr>
<tr><td>Repairing
Pipe for sink
Doctor-sick visit
Repairman-refrigerator
Teeth cleaning

Machines (Technology)
Cell phone
Flash drive
Cable TV
Internet Service

Having Fun
Monopoly game
Movie tickets
Video rental
Popcorn

Health
Apples
Soup
Prescription</td></tr>
<tr><td colspan="3">Possible Generalizations (Step 5): People use money to take care of home and people, and to have fun and relax. Money helps us get products we need and products we want.</td></tr>
</table>

Lesson Plan: *Concept Development*
Grade Level: *Secondary*
Purpose of Discussion: *To extend and clarify students' concept of* To Kill a Mockingbird
Background Information for Lesson: To Kill a Mockingbird
Note: *This is the first of two lessons based on the same novel. This lesson uses a list of characters; the next lesson is based on a list of events. Compare the two to see both the differences and the similarities.*

Concept Development	*Focusing Questions*	*Materials and Supports*
Step 1: List	*Who are the characters in* To Kill a Mockingbird?	• Make sure students have their book available. • Assign character list for homework the night before.
Step 2: Group and Label	<u>Grouping:</u> *Which of these characters share something meaningful in common?* <u>Labeling:</u> *What name can we give to this group? Why do you think that is a good label for this group?*	• Provide rules for grouping: five groups with four characters in each group. • Record answers in the second column of the chart. • Change marker colors so students can follow the progression of ideas.
Step 3: Subsume	*Who on our list could fit in more than one of our groups? Why do you think (x) fits in this group?* *Which character(s) could also go in to the group we called (y)?* *Which of the groups could fit inside another group?* *How could we adjust the name of a group so that it would be broad enough to include another group?* Summary Question: *What are some of the ideas that are emerging based on our first set of groups and the relationships you see between them?*	• Use the third section of the chart. • Use tree map format to demonstrate relationships. • Change marker color. • Have students support ideas using text where necessary.
Step 4: Regroup	*You've done a great job so far! Let's set these groups aside and try to find three new ways to group the characters. Try to put three characters in each group.*	• Provide a short timeline to increase on-task behavior. • Provide encouragement for students who are struggling to find new ideas. • Allow students to refer to the book to get ideas.
Step 5: Generalize	*Thinking about our entire conversation, including the list, all of our groups and labels, and the hierarchy we created by subsuming groups, what are some messages that come to us through the characters in* To Kill a Mockingbird?	• Allow students a minute to think and write down their ideas before discussing the generalizations. • Gather several ideas before beginning discussion.

Cognitive Map for Concept Development

Purpose of Discussion: *To extend and clarify students' understanding of characters in* To Kill a Mockingbird.

Possible List (Step 1)	*Possible Groups and Labels (Step 2)*	*Possible Subsuming (Step 3)*
1. Scout 2. Jem 3. Dill 4. Atticus 5. Uncle Jack 6. Cousin Francis 7. Maudie 8. Calpurnia 9. Zeke 10. Tom Robinson 11. Mayella Ewell 12. Bob Ewell 13. Walter Cunninham 14. Dad Cunningham 15. Stephanie Crawford 16. Mrs. Dubois 17. Miss Rachel 18. Miss Caroline 19. Dolphus Raymond 20. Mr. Underwood 21. Heck Tate 22. Arthur (Boo) Radley 23. Helen Robinson 24. Reverend Sykes 25. Nathan Radley 26. Ms. Merriweather 27. Cecil Jacobs 28. Aunt Alexandra	Maycomb Children Scout Jem Walter C. Cecil Jacobs Fitch Neighbors Crawford Dubois Rachel Maudie Boo Radley Town Workers Underwood Heck Tate N Radley Reverend Sykes African Americans Tom Robinson Helen Robinson Calpurnia Zeke Poor People Mayella Ewell Bob Ewell Walter C. Dolphus Ray-mond Fitches Aunt Alexandra Cousin Frances Atticus Uncle Jack	Town Workers Underwood Heck Tate N. Radley Reverend Sykes Poor People Fitches African Americans Fitch Neighbors Children Town Workers Poor People African Americans *Possible Regroups and Labels (Step 4)* Scout's Teachers Atticus Calpurnia Miss Maudie Aunt Alexandra Miss Caroline Change Perspective Jem Scout Walter C. Atticus Traditional Values Cousin Francis Aunt Alexandra Ms. Merri-weather Mockingbirds/ Outcasts Boo Radley Mayella Dill Dolphus Scout Tom

Possible Generalizations (Step 5): People are not as simple as they seem. Understanding leads to change.

Cognitive Map format adapted from the Institute for Staff Development (1971).

Lesson Plan: *Concept Development*
Grade Level: *Secondary*
Purpose of Discussion: *To extend and clarify students' concept of* To Kill a Mockingbird
Background Information for Lesson: To Kill a Mockingbird

Concept Development	*Focusing Questions*	*Materials and Supports*
Step 1: List	*What are some of the key events in the novel* To Kill a Mockingbird? *What made you select this as an important event?* *Why do you think (x) is important?* *Think through the entire story; look in the book if necessary.*	• Give students time in pairs to create a list of events. • Make sure students have their book available.
Step 2: Group and Label	Grouping: *Which of these events could be grouped in a way that gives us a sense of what the book is about?* Labeling: *What would be a good two- to three-word label for this group?* *How did you come up with that label?*	• Provide rules for grouping: five groups with four items in each group. • Record answers in the second column of the chart. • Change marker colors so students can follow the progression of ideas.
Step 3: Subsume	*Which of the events in one group could also fit in another group?* *Which group could be a subset of another group? Why do you think (x) fits as a subset of (y)?*	• Use the third section of the chart. • Ask students to support their ideas. • Encourage students to create new labels to subsume groups if necessary.
Step 4: Regroup	*Put the groups and labels we just discussed aside for the moment, and find three new ways to group the items on our list, thinking not only about finding an original group, but also about our goal of gaining insight into the novel.*	• Provide a short time limit. • Keep an upbeat demeanor to encourage students who are struggling to find new ideas. • Suggest that students find three new groups with three items each.
Step 5: Generalize	*Gathering together all of the information from our conversation today, from the initial list all the way to our last groups, what are some general lessons we can take away from* To Kill a Mockingbird? *What do you think the book says about people in broader terms?*	• Develop three generalizations. • Have students create a tree map using one generalization for homework.

Cognitive Map for Concept Development

Purpose of Discussion: *To extend and clarify students' understanding of events in* To Kill a Mockingbird

Possible List (Step 1)	*Possible Groups and Labels (Step 2)*	*Possible Subsuming (Step 3)*
1. Scout meets Dill 2. Scout is told not to read 3. Scout rides tire to Boo's house 4. Tree trunk presents 5. Tree trunk filled 6. Jem reads to Ms. Dubois 7. Jem and Scout go to church with Calpurnia 8. Christmas fight with Frances 9. Fight with Cecil at school 10. Walter Cunningham has lunch with Scout and Jem 11. Dill runs away 12. Drinking coke with Mr. Dolphus 13. Atticus shoots a mad dog 14. Ms. Maudie's house burns 15. Boo gives Scout a blanket 16. Atticus protects Tom outside jailhouse 17. Tom can't put his hand on the bible 18. Men come to Fitch house 19. Heck Tate visits Atticus about Tom Robinson 20. Coffee with Aunt Alexandra 21. Bob Ewell attacks Scout and Jem 22. Tom Robinson is shot 23. Scout, Jem, and Dill watch trial from balcony 24. Scout walks Boo home 25. Jem has to rescue pants, finds them sewn 26. Boo stabs Bob Ewell	<u>Boo</u> • Scout rides tire to Boo's house • Tree trunk presents • Boo gives Scout a blanket • Jem has to rescue pants, finds them sewn <u>Changed Impressions</u> • Jem reads to Ms. Dubois • Atticus shoots a mad dog • Scout walks Boo home • Walter Cunningham has lunch with Scout and Jem • Drinking coke with Mr. Dolphus • Coffee with Aunt Alexandra <u>Crossing Line</u> • Scout is told not to read • Scout and Jem go to church with Calpurnia • Dill runs away • Drinking coke with Mr. Dolphus • Atticus defends Tom Robinson <u>Tom Robinson (TR)</u> • TR is shot • Atticus protects TR outside jail • Heck visits Atticus about TR • Men come to Fitch house <u>Scout Fights</u> • Fight with Cecil at school • Fight with • Frances • Fight with • Walter Cunningham	<u>Changed Impressions</u> • Jem reads to Ms. Dubois • Atticus shoots a mad dog • Scout walks Boo home • Walter Cunningham has lunch with Scout and Jem • Drinking coke with Mr. Dolphus • Coffee with Aunt Alexandra <u>Boo</u> <u>Scout fights</u> ***Possible Regroups and Labels (Step 4)*** <u>Tragedies</u> Ms. Maudie's house burns Tom Robinson is shot Bob Ewell attacks Scout and Jem <u>Surprises/Insights</u> Attitcus shoots a mad dog Coffee with Aunt Alexandra Jem and Scout go to church with Calpurnia Jem reads to Ms. Dubois <u>Boo Instructs</u> Jem has to rescue pants (Jem) Boo gives Scout a blanket (Scout) Tree trunk presents (Jem/Scout)

Possible Generalizations (Step 5): *There is more to people than meets the eye. A lot can be learned by listening and talking to other people. Big things happen even in small towns. Opportunities to learn come from everywhere and everyone. Tolerance is a result of becoming familiar with something or someone.*

Cognitive Map format adapted from the Institute for Staff Development (1971).

Lesson Plan: *Concept Development*
Grade Level: *Secondary*
Purpose of Discussion: *To extend and clarify students' concept of events leading to conflict/war*
Background Information for Lesson: *Textbook information, research notes, lecture*

Concept Development	*Focusing Questions*	*Materials and Supports*
Step 1: List	*Based on your reading, research, and notes, what are some of the events that led the nation to Civil War?*	• Make sure students have their book available.
Step 2: Group	Grouping: *Which items this list share an important characteristic?* Labeling: *What is the most accurate label for this group?* *Why do you think (x) is a good label?*	• Provide rules for grouping: five groups with four items in each group. • Ask students for justification. • Record answers in the second column of the chart. • Change marker colors so students can follow the progression of ideas.
Step 3: Subsume	*Which group could fit underneath another group? What do these groups share in common?* *Which groups, if any, could be a subset of another group?* Summary Question: *What ideas about the Civil War are beginning to emerge?*	• Use the third section of the chart. • Change marker color. • Allow students to subsume in small groups and share their hierarchies with each other.
Step 4: Regroup	*You've done a great job so far! Let's set these groups aside and try to find three new ways to group these events. Try to create three new groups with at least four items each.*	• Provide a short timeline to increase on-task behavior. • Provide encouragement for students who are struggling to find new ideas. • Allow students to refer to the book to get ideas.
Step 5: Generalize	*Thinking about our entire conversation, including the list, all of our groups and labels, and the hierarchy we created by subsuming groups, what are can we say in general about the causes of the Civil War?*	• Allow students a minute to think and write down their ideas before discussing the generalizations. • Gather several ideas before beginning discussion.

Cognitive Map for Concept Development
Purpose of Discussion: *To extend and clarify students' understanding of events leading to the Civil War*

<table>
<tr><th>Possible List (Step 1)</th><th>Possible Groups and Labels (Step 2)</th><th>Possible Subsuming (Step 3)</th></tr>
<tr>
<td rowspan="3">1. Fugitive Slave Act
2. Uncle Tom's Cabin
3. Kansas-Nebraska Act
4. Dred Scott
5. Harpers Ferry
6. Lincoln elected
7. Lincoln Douglass Debates
8. Compromise of 1850
9. Underground railroad
10. Cotton gin
11. Missouri Compromise
12. Louisiana Purchase
13. Bleeding Kansas
14. Declaration of the Causes of Secession
15. Fort Sumter
16. Plantation economy
17. Slave trade profitable—molasses, rum, slaves triangle
18. Fredrick Douglass biography
19. Jefferson Davis elected
20. South Carolina seceded
21. Nat Turner Rebellion
22. Charles Sumner attacked in Congress
23. Kansas enters Union as free state
24. Confederate Congress authorizes an army
25. Confederate constitution accepted</td>
<td rowspan="3"><u>Slave Rebellion</u>
Underground railroad
Harpers Ferry
Nat Turner Rebellion
Uncle Tom's Cabin

<u>Government Changes</u>
Jefferson Davis elected
South Carolina seceded
Lincoln elected
Lincoln Douglass Debates

<u>Legislation</u>
Kansas-Nebraska Act
Dred Scott
Fugitive Slave Act
Missouri Compromise
Compromise of 1850

<u>Southern Economy</u>
Cotton gin
Cotton price
Slave trade profitable</td>
<td><u>Government Changes</u>
Jefferson Davis elected
South Carolina seceded
Lincoln elected
Lincoln Douglas Debates
South Carolina seceded
<u>Legislation</u></td>
</tr>
<tr><th>Possible Regroups and Labels (Step 4)</th></tr>
<tr><td><u>Uprising</u>
Harpers Ferry
Nat Turner
Underground Railroad
SC seceded

<u>Breaking Apart</u>
Declaration of Secession
Jefferson Davis elected president
Sumner attacked in Congress
Confederate Congress authorizes an army

<u>Publications</u>
Uncle Tom's Cabin
Fredrick Douglass biography
Lincoln Douglass Debates
Confederate Constitution

<u>Midwest Issues</u>
Missouri Compromise
Louisiana Purchase
Bleeding Kansas/Kansas enters as free state
Kansas-Nebraska Act</td></tr>
<tr><td colspan="3">Possible Generalizations (Step 5) : The Civil War was caused by social, economic, and government upheaval. Events across the nation contributed to the Civil War.</td></tr>
</table>

Lesson Plan: *Concept Development*
Grade Level: *Secondary*
Purpose of Discussion: *To extend and clarify students' concept of graphs/numerical representation*
Background Information for Lesson: *Graphs students find in the media and bring to class*

Concept Development	*Focusing Questions*	*Materials and Supports*
Step 1: List	*Based on the graphs in front of you, what do you know about graphs?* *What do they look like?* *Where are they used?* *What other information do you see?*	• Post graphs on a bulletin board, and give students time to look at them and gather ideas for the list before starting the discussion.
Step 2: Group and Label	Grouping: *What groups can you form to show a similarity shared by a subset of items?* *Why do you think (x) belongs this group?* Labeling: *What label best describes what this group has in common?*	• Provide rules for grouping: five groups with four items in each group. • Record answers in the second column of the chart. • Change marker colors so students can follow the progression of ideas.
Step 3: Subsume	*We put (x) in this group. What other group could it go in?* *Which group could fit inside another group?* *Why would you put (x) in that group?*	• Use the third section of the chart. • Change marker color. • Record hierarchies as an outline or a tree map.
Step 4: Regroup	*So far, this has been kind of easy! Now, go back and find brand new categories to use to group items on the list.*	• Provide a short timeline to promote on-task behavior. • Provide encouragement for students who are struggling to find new ideas. • Suggest that students find three new groups with three items each.
Step 5: Generalize	*Based on our discussion and looking at the different groups, what are some things we can say in general about the uses of graphs?* *What information did you use as the basis of our general statement?* *Which of these statements mean nearly the same thing? Which could go together?*	• Allow students a minute to think and share ideas with a partner before beginning discussion.

Cognitive Map for Concept Development
Purpose of Discussion: *To extend and clarify students' concept of graphs/numerical representation*

<table>
<tr><th>Possible List (Step 1)</th><th>Possible Groups and Labels (Step 2)</th><th>Possible Subsuming (Step 3)</th></tr>
<tr><td rowspan="3">1. Bar graphs
2. Quadratic
3. Circle graph
4. Line graph
5. X coordinate
6. Y coordinate
7. Leaf
8. Scatterplot
9. Stock market
10. Dentists use (brand) toothpaste
11. Voting patterns
12. Increase in wages
13. Legend
14. Student height
15. Calories in fast food
16. Pictograph
17. Mortgage rates
18. Source of information
19. Numbers
20. Costs of rides
21. Scale
22. Population age
23. Data
24. Stem</td><td rowspan="3"><u>Graph Types</u>
Bar
Circle
Line
Pictograph
Quadratic
Scatterplot

<u>Terms</u>
Data
Leaf
Scale
Stem

<u>Graph Elements</u>
Legend
Source
X coordinate
Y coordinate
Numbers

<u>Information Reported</u>
Mortgage rate
Cost of rides
Increase in wages
Stock market

<u>People Patterns</u>
Dentists use (brand) tooth-paste
Voting patterns
Population age
Student height</td><td><u>Graph Types</u>
Terms

<u>Information Reported</u>
People Patterns</td></tr>
<tr><td>Possible Regroups and Labels (Step 4)</td></tr>
<tr><td><u>Money-Related</u>
Stock market
Mortgage rates
Cost of rides
Increase in wages

<u>Chunked Data</u>
Scatterplot
Bar graph
Circle graph
Histogram
Pictograph

<u>Trends Up or Down</u>
Stock market
Voting patterns
Increase in wages
Mortgage rates

<u>Helps Interpreting</u>
Title
Legend
Numbers</td></tr>
<tr><td colspan="3">Possible Generalization (Step Five): Graphs structure numbers to describe how people and things change. Graphs have shapes to present information in chunks or trends.</td></tr>
</table>

Cognitive Map format adapted from Institute for Staff Development (1971).

Lesson Plan: *Concept Development*
Grade Level: *Secondary*
Purpose of Discussion: *To extend and clarify students' concept of literature*
Background Information for Lesson: *Works of literature, research on elements of literature*

Concept Development	*Focusing Questions*	*Materials and Supports*
Step 1: List	*What are some of the words we've used to describe different aspects of literature?*	• Give students time to write down a few ideas. • Remind students to refer to the textbook for ideas.
Step 2: Group and Label	Grouping: *Which of these elements of literature go together because they are alike in some way?* *Why do you think (x) belongs in this group?* Labeling: *What would be a good title for this group?*	• Provide rules for grouping: five groups with four items in each group. • Record answers in the second column of the chart • Change marker colors so students can follow the progression of ideas.
Step 3: Subsume	*What other group could (x) go in? Why?* *Where else might (y) fit?*	• Change marker color. • Use the third section of the chart; write ideas in outline format so students see the hierarchy
Step 4: Regroup	*Now that we have a basic set of groups, let's push a little further. Create at least three new groups with at least three items each. Make sure your groups are both new and relevant to our discussion of literature.*	• Provide a short timeline to promote on-task behavior. • Provide encouragement for students who are struggling to find new ideas.
Step 5: Generalize	*Based on our discussion and looking at the different groups and labels, what are some general statements we can make about the structure and function of literature?*	• Assign initial generalizations as homework. • Integrate ideas into two or three statements. • Post statements on bulletin board, and allow students to list additional novels that fit the generalizations.

Cognitive Map for Concept Development
Purpose of Discussion: *To extend and clarify students' concept of literature*

Possible List (Step 1)	*Possible Groups and Labels (Step 2)*	*Possible Subsuming (Step 3)*
1. Imagery 2. Tone 3. Theme 4. Irony 5. Characterization 6. Plot 7. Style 8. Allusion 9. Figurative language 10. Mood 11. Setting 12. Dialogue 13. Flashback 14. Internal conflict 15. External conflict 16. Persona 17. Foil 18. Foreshadow 19. Symbolism 20. Protagonist 21. Antagonist 22. Climax 23. Motif 24. Flat character 25. Dynamic character 26. Round character	<u>Basic Elements</u> Setting Plot Characterization Mood Theme <u>Character Elements</u> Persona Flat character Dynamic character Round character <u>Indirect Messages</u> Allusion Figurative language Flashback Symbolism <u>Emotional Power</u> Mood Motif Foreshadow Irony Symbolism <u>Initiate Change</u> Internal conflict External conflict Antagonist Foil Dialogue	<u>Basic Elements</u> Character Elements Initiate Change <u>Indirect Messages</u> Emotional Power ***Possible Regrouping and Labels (Step 4)*** <u>Deeper Meaning</u> Figurative language Allusion Irony Symbolism <u>Varying Time</u> Foreshadow Flashback Setting <u>Pervasive Threads</u> Theme Symbolism Motif <u>O'Henry Style</u> Surprise ending Irony Climax

Possible Generalizations (Step 5): *A work of literature is a story with a deeper meaning. Literature presents stories about characters moving through and sometimes changing with time. Authors can define their style by using different elements of literature.*

Cognitive Map format adapted from the Institute for Staff Development (1971).

Lesson Plan: *Concept Development*
Grade Level: *Secondary*
Purpose of Discussion: *To extend and clarify students' concept of the Civil Rights movement, 1950s–1970s*
Background Information for Lesson: *Textbook, classroom resources, research notes*

Note: *This model lesson is ideal for advanced students. Notice that students go back to subsuming again after regrouping, and at the end of this lesson, students are encouraged create universal abstract generalizations.*

Concept Development	*Focusing Questions*	*Materials and Supports*
Step 1: List	*What are some of the pivotal events that occurred during the Civil Rights movement of the late 1950s–early 1970s?*	• Remind students to bring completed worksheet to class for this lesson. • Allow a two-minute data search before gathering information for the list.
Step 2: Group and Label	<u>Grouping:</u> *Which of these go together because they are alike in some way?* *Why do you think (x) belongs in this group?* <u>Labeling:</u> *Thinking about the reasons why you put these together, what would be some good names for your groups?* *What name would you give this group?*	• Provide rules for grouping: five groups with four items in each group. • Record answers in the second column of the chart. • Change marker colors so students can follow the progression of ideas.
Step 3: Subsume	*What other group could (x) go in? Why?* *Where else might (y) fit? How is it that (y) could belong to both groups?* Summary Question: *What are some ideas you see emerging based on what is on the board right now?*	• Use the third section of the chart. • Change marker color. • Ask students for justification. • Write summary statements in a corner of the chart.
Step 4: Regrouping	*So far, so good! Now let's put these first groups aside and find three other new groups that reveal something different about the Civil Rights movement.* *How would you incorporate these new ideas into the hierarchy we created in the last step?*	• Use the fourth column of the chart; change marker color. • Give students an initial five-minute time limit; add time as necessary. • Suggest that students find four new groups with three items each. • Circle or box the labels from Step 2 so students remember that they are off limits.
Step 5: Generalize	Homework: *Write a generalization about America during the Civil Rights movement based on all of the ideas we've discussed. Include a one-paragraph justification that draws a connection between your generalization and the ideas and facts we've discussed today.* In class: *Let's use your ideas to create a statement that does not directly mention the Civil Rights movement but describes related human behaviors more generally.*	• Assign the first generalization for homework. Briefly discuss them the next day in class. • Give students an example of increasingly abstract generalizations: *My dog Sporty loves to chase a ball.* to *Many dogs seem to enjoy chasing objects.* to *Many animals chase objects.*

Cognitive Map for Concept Development
Purpose of Discussion: *To extend and clarify students' understanding of the Civil Rights movement.*

Possible List (Step 1)	*Possible Groups and Labels (Step 2)*	*Possible Subsuming* (Step 3)*
1. *Brown v. Board of Education* 2. Southern Manifesto urges resistance to desegregation 3. Little Rock Central High School desegregated 4. Montgomery bus boycott 5. Freedom Riders oppose segregation 6. James Meredith enrolls at the University of Mississippi 7. Desegregation drive in Birmingham 8. *Letter from Birmingham Jail* 9. Gov. Wallace stops integration of the University of Alabama 10. Medgar Evers murdered 11. March on Washington 12. Bombing of Birmingham church 13. 24th Amendment passed 14. Civil Rights Act of 1964 (discrim.) 15. Civil Rights Act of 1968 (housing) 16. Mississippi Summer Freedom Project 17. Selma to Montgomery march 18. Voting Rights Act approved 19. Watts Riots 20. *Loving v. Virginia*: interracial marriage 21. Malcolm X assassinated 22. Executive Order 11246 23. Race riots in Detroit and Newark 24. Martin Luther King, Jr., assassinated 25. Greensboro sit-in	<u>Violence</u> Watts Riots Race riots in Detroit and Newark Bombing at Birmingham church <u>Education Rights</u> *Brown v. Board of Education* Governor Wallace stops integration of U. of Alabama James Meredith enrolls in University of Mississippi Desegregation of Little Rock High School <u>Voting Rights</u> M.S. Summer Freedom Project 24th Amendment passed Selma to Montgomery march Voting Rights Act approved <u>Non-Violent Action</u> Montgomery bus boycott Greensboro sit-in March on Washington Freedom Riders *Letter from Birmingham Jail* <u>Lost Leaders</u> M. L. King assassinated Medgar Evers murdered Malcolm X assassinated	**ACTION** <u>Non-Violent Action</u> Voting Rights *LEGAL ACTION* <u>Violence</u> Lost Leaders *TRADITION RESISTS* <u>NATIONAL MOVEMENT</u> SOUTHERN U.S. ***Possible Regroups and Labels (Step 4)*** <u>Tradition Resists</u> Southern Manifesto Governor Wallace stops integration of U of Alabama Medgar Evers assassinated Bombing at Birmingham church <u>Legal Action</u> Civil Rights act of 1964 Voting Rights Act of 1965 *Brown v. Board of Education* 24th Amendment passed *Loving v. Virginia* <u>Southern U.S.</u> Greensboro, **NC**, sit-in Integration of Little Rock, **AR**, HS Selma to Montgomery, **AL**, march James Meredith enrolls at U. **Miss.** <u>National Movement</u> March on Washington Watts Riots Riots in Detroit and Newark Freedom Riders

Possible First-Level Generalizations (Step 5): *The Civil Rights movement was marked by conflict and resistance to change. The Civil Rights movement was national, not Southern.*
Possible Second-Level Generalizations: *Change requires action. Change can create opposing action. Citizen protest requires strong leaders willing to take personal risks.*

**Capitals represent the second level of subsuming; bold represents a high-level label.*

Cognitive Map format adapted from the Institute for Staff Development (1971).

CHAPTER 7: IMPROVING QUESTIONING THROUGH DISCUSSION ANALYSIS

> *A curriculum which stresses active leaning...requires a teaching strategy which relies heavily on asking questions. If the development of autonomy in thinking is an important objective, questions (or the "seeking" functions) of teaching are vastly more important than the "giving" functions.*
>
> *Focusing is needed because students, as well as adults, tend to indulge in associative thinking (branch off on a word or phrase in a preceding statement) and, therefore, make irrational transitions from on aspect of the topic to another....* (Taba 1967. pp. 79-80)

Leading a discussion is like conducting an orchestra. With an encouraging phrase, students are welcomed to join in; the pitch of the conversation rises with a controversial question or calms with a moment to reflect. Like conductors, skilled discussion leaders are constantly attuned to the pulse of their "orchestra."

Conductors are also highly attuned to their own actions. If the baton goes awry, the audience may hear tubas instead of piccolos, or a fugue may take on the tempo of a jazz riff. Similarly, instructors must be aware not only of their students' comments, *but also of their own*. Much of the success of a discussion rides on considered judgments about which questions to ask, which ideas to pursue in depth, and which way to turn when questions run amuck.

Developing the ability to self-monitor while teaching, attending to what you say and how you say it, first requires having a way to observe and reflect on your own teaching practice. Taba (and others like Ted Parsons, 1969) pioneered work both in defining the qualities of effective classroom discussion and in developing materials to help teachers cultivate these qualities. The materials developed by Taba and her colleagues were originally designed to accompany her strategies, but they are more generally useful to: 1) *individuals* seeking to refine their technique, 2) *peer coaching groups* seeking a productive focus of conversation, and 3) *teacher mentors or administrators* seeking a source of measurable, observable, meaningful improvement in instruction.

This section presents a new interpretation of two components of a larger body of materials that take teachers into systematically deeper layers of self-awareness and sophistication in classroom discussion. These first two steps include: 1) learning to identify patterns in classroom conversation, and 2) distinguishing between closed, open, and focused questions.

DISCUSSION ANALYSIS: PATTERNS IN CLASSROOM CONVERSATION

Interaction is fundamental to classroom discussion, so it stands to reason, then, that the first step in becoming a skilled discussion leader is recognizing patterns of classroom conversation. How often do you ask questions? What kinds of questions do you ask? How often do you give information? How often do your students talk to you? To each other? Do your classroom management strategies help or intrude on learning time? Self-assessment of this sort requires finding a way to watch your teaching in action. Fortunately, any teacher who owns a web cam, video camera, or even a cell phone can capture both audio and video records of her class.

Observing and Recording Patterns in Classroom Interaction

The first step in identifying elements of classroom interaction is to convert classroom conversation into a code that will reveal meaningful patterns. Eventually it will be helpful to look at interaction in close detail; however, it is helpful at the start to take a global look at conversation patterns by separating conversations into three parts:

Talking (T): any statement that gives information or tells something directly related to the lesson.

Asking (A): any questions asked, unless the question is related to classroom management such as "Can I get some water?"

Management (M): any classroom management, whether question or statement. This includes any conversation outside of instruction, such as passing out papers, organizing students into groups, discipline issues, etc. Positive or negative reinforcement (*"Good job!"* or *"Nice try!"*) should also be coded M since it is not directly related to instruction, but telling a student whether he/she is correct or incorrect is coded as Talking.

Each statement in the coded conversation is recorded in order on the Discussion Analysis form. The Discussion Analysis form is simply two rows of boxes: one row for teacher statements, and one for student statements:

Teacher										
Students										

When a box in one row is marked, the opposing box above or below is left blank. This makes the pattern of interaction between teacher and students clearer to see. This brief interaction serves as an example:

Teacher: *What is 2+2?*

Erin: *Is it 4?*

Teacher: *The answer is 4. Good job!*

When coded and recorded on the Discussion Analysis form, the conversation looks like this:

Teacher	A		T	M
Students		A		

The interaction has four statements, so four boxes are filled. "The answer is 4" and "Good job!" are treated as separate entries. Treating individual statements separately provides a means of determining if a teacher—or a student—is dominating classroom conversation. Adding a subscript to the student entries can distinguish between students, if desired.

A comparison of three brief classroom conversations demonstrates how different patterns emerge when comments are coded and transferred to the Discussion Analysis form. The teachers in these three hypothetical classes are all in the listing phase of the same Concept Development lesson. Fourteen comments from each conversation are coded.

Classroom A

Teacher:	*What kinds of graphs have you gathered in your research?*
Scott:	*I have one that is either a circle or pie graph.*
Teacher:	*Circle or graph? Scott, do you know?*
Scott:	*Circle.*
Sophia:	*No, it's called a pie graph.*
Teacher:	*It's a pie graph. It has sections just like a pie. What are some other kinds of graphs?*
Ethan:	*I found a line graph.*
Teacher:	*Line graph.*
Brittany:	*I think mine is a bar graph.*
Teacher:	*Let me see. That's called a box-and-whiskers graph.*

DISCUSSION ANALYSIS GRID FOR TEACHER A

Teacher	A	T_1	A	A	T_1	T_2	T	T	A	T_3	T	T_4	M	T
Students														

Classroom B

Teacher:	*What kinds of graphs have you gathered in your research? Did anyone find a circle graph?*
Kelsey:	*Yes, I did.*
Teacher:	*It's also called a pie chart, right? It's got segments that look just like a pie. Now let's hear from someone else. I want to hear from someone who doesn't have a pie chart. Did anyone bring in a line graph? Tyler, did you?*
Tyler:	*Yes.*
Teacher:	*Megan, what did you bring in?*
Megan:	*I think mine's a bar graph.*
Teacher:	*No, that's not a bar graph. Does any know what that is?*

GRID FOR TEACHER B

Teacher	A	A		A	T	T	T	A	A		A		T	A
Students			T_1							T_2		T_3		

Classroom C

Teacher:	*What kinds of graphs have you gathered in your research?*
Scott:	*I have one that is either a circle or pie graph.*
Teacher:	*Which is it, Scott?*
Scott:	*Circle.*
Sophia:	*No, it's called a pie graph.*
Teacher:	*Scott, Sophia, look that up in the book please, and let us know what you find. (To class) What other kinds of graphs did you find?*
Darius:	*Line graph.*
Megan:	*I think mine is a bar graph.*
Teacher:	*What makes you uncertain?*
Megan:	*Well, it has these little lines coming out of the top and bottom.*
Teacher	*(Showing Megan's graph to the class) Who knows what kind of graph this is?*
Tyler:	*It's a box-and-whisker!*
Scott:	*I found the name of our graph; it's a pie chart.*

GRID FOR TEACHER C

Teacher	A		A			M	A			A		A		
Students		T_1		T_1	T_2			T_3	T_4		T_4		T_5	T_1

Summary Statistics

Classroom A		Classroom B		Classroom C	
Teacher	***Students***	***Teacher***	***Students***	***Teacher***	***Students***
Talk 4	Talk 5	Talk 4	Talk 3	Talk 0	Talk 8
Ask 4	Ask 0	Ask 7	Ask 0	Ask 5	Ask 0
Manage 1	Manage 0	Manage 0	Manage 0	Manage 1	Manage 0
Total 9	***Total 5***	***Total 11***	***Total 3***	***Total 6***	***Total 8***

Interpreting Patterns in Classroom Conversation

The grids and the summary table reveal very different patterns. Although the teacher in Classroom B asks the most questions, it is the least interactive. Most of the questions she asks are closed, and she sometimes doesn't seem to need an answer to her questions at all. The pattern in Classroom A shows some interaction taking place, yet the teacher seems to have some habits he might want to change, such as asking unnecessary questions and giving information when he could involve the class by asking them for information. The teacher in Classroom C speaks less frequently than her students and has more students engaged in the conversation. She asks fewer questions than the teacher in Classroom B, but more of her students participate. She seems to understand when a question could be substituted for a statement, opening the classroom to broader engagement and participation.

COMMON PATTERNS IN CLASSROOM INTERACTION

Patterns in the Discussion Analysis are not inherently bad or good; they simply point to areas that warrant deeper examination. Some patterns that lead to fruitful self-analysis include:

Two or more A's in a row: A string of two or more A's in the Teacher row suggests rapid-fire or repetitive questioning, which can be intimidating or confusing to students. Consecutive A's might also suggest that a teacher rephrased a question to make it clearer.

An A and T together in the Teacher row: This pattern suggests rhetorical questions or a question that a teacher both asked and answered.

No Student entries: An inquiry-based lesson should feature a constant interchange between teacher and student. When the Discussion Analysis form has no entries on the Student row, there is no discussion.

No Student A's: An absence of A's in the Student row suggests a conversation in which only the teacher is asking questions. This could either be a sign of an active exchange in which students are contributing many ideas, or a classroom environment where students do not feel free to ask questions of their own.

Several Student T's in a row: When many students talk without asking anything, students may be excitedly sharing ideas, or they may be talking over each other instead of taking time to listen to their classmates.

CLOSED, OPEN, AND FOCUSED QUESTIONS

All questions, with one exception, are requests for information. Learning distinctions between different types of questions is the next step to effective classroom questioning. Three forms of questions common to classrooms are closed, open, and focused.

Closed questions: Closed questions have limited scope, having only one right answer. They are often directed to a single student, restricting the opportunity for discussion. Closed questions are not "bad"; indeed, they are essential to fact-checking. However, excessive use of closed questions can train students in limited right-or-wrong thinking and removes valuable opportunities to analyze, speculate, empathize, or ponder. Closed questions rarely, if ever, lead to higher-order thinking.

Subcategories of closed questions include:

> *Yes or no questions:* ["Do you think...," "Is this...," "Are you..." are all typical openers for yes/no questions. These questions can stop a conversation in its tracks with one word: "No".]
>
> *Single right-answer questions:* ["In what year did Columbus discover America?" "What is the third planet of the Solar System?" "What is the name of the rat in *Charlotte's Web*?" These questions have a single right answer; they raise no curiosity and evoke no thinking other than recall.]
>
> *Rhetorical questions:* [Rhetorical questions are questions that either: 1) have an answer embedded: "2+2=4, right?" or 2) are immediately answered by the asker: "What's 2+2? 4!" or are asked without expectation of an answer: "Isn't math wonderful?"]

Open-Ended Questions: Open-ended questions have many possible answers, invite participation from many respondents, and often lead to more questions. Research on open questions gives evidence that they contribute to high levels of classroom engagement, as well as higher-order thinking. Questions that start with "*Is it*" or "*Can it*," "*Does it*" or "*Will it*" are nearly always closed. Questions that start with "*Which*" or "*Why*" are more likely to be open.

Even small changes can open questions and send subtle messages to students that they are supposed to participate in the conversation and that you expect them to think beyond a "yes" or "no" answer. The chart on the next page shows how some typically closed questions can be converted to open questions.

Open-Ended Versions of Common Closed Questions

Closed Question	***Open Question***	***Benefit***
Can you add 2+2?	Who can add 2+2?	The open question communicates the assumption that someone can add 2+2.
Is it brown?	What color is it?	The open question requires students to pay attention, sort through options, and select a response. The closed question requires much less attention or engagement.
Do you think plants get food from the sun?	How many of you think plants get food from the sun?	The closed question can be answered by an individual; the rephrased question requires participation from the entire class.
Is there any benefit?	What, if any, are the benefits?	Students can simply reply "No" to the closed question, necessitating follow-up. The open question has room for the "No" answer but also cues students to consider other possibilities.
What is the answer?	What are some possible answers?	The open question assumes there is more than one possible answer and automatically invites more students to participate.
John Steinbeck wrote *East of Eden*, didn't he?	Who wrote *East of Eden*?	Rhetorical questions send the tacit message that students do not need to answer—or even attend to—questions.

Focused Questions: Focused questions are a subset of open-ended questions, and they are perhaps the most important kind of question to master for effective classroom discussion. Focused questions are distinguished by their ability to point students in a productive direction. Consider these two open-ended questions:

What did you see in the film about polar bears?

What did you notice about how polar bears live?

Both of the questions are open-ended. However, the first question allows too many answers, including answers that may not be helpful or relevant, like "the sun" or "the title." The second question is both open-ended and focused; it points students in a direction and puts boundaries around appropriate responses.

Open, Focused and Closed Questions

Open	Focused	Closed
What were the effects of the Civil War?	What were the effects of the Civil War on Southern economy?	What was the price of cotton after the Civil War?
What did you notice in the reading?	What did the reading say about how plants grow?	Where do you put the roots of a plant?
What are examples of risk taking?	What are examples of risks we take in everyday life?	Is crossing the road without looking an example of a risk?
What are the most important American cities?	What American cities have the largest populations?	Which American city has the largest population?

DISCUSSION ANALYSIS AND CLOSED OR OPEN QUESTIONS

The Discussion Analysis form can help develop awareness of the kinds of questions asked most frequently. The pattern is revealed by simply going back and putting an X over every A on the grid that represents a closed question and a circle around every A that is an open question. This second layer of analysis adds another perspective to some differences in Classrooms A, B, and C.

Teacher A	(A)		AX	(A)			T	T	(A)		T		M	T
Students		T_1			T_1	T_2				T_3		T_4		

Teacher B	~~A~~	~~A~~		~~A~~	T	T	T	~~A~~	~~A~~		A		T	~~A~~
Students			T_1							T_2		T_3		

Teacher C	(A)		(A)			M	(A)			(A)		(A)		
Students		T_1		T_1	T_2			T_3	T_4		T_4		T_5	T_1

Teacher B asks more questions than either Teachers A or C, but all of her questions are closed. Even the questions that seem open-ended, like "What kinds of graphs have you gathered in your research?" end up being rhetorical because she does not give students a chance to respond. Teacher A asks both open and closed questions, and he could be encouraged to look back at his questions to see whether his closed questions could be opened. Teacher C asks more questions than Teacher A, and her questions are all open.

Classroom A		**Classroom B**		**Classroom C**	
Teacher	***Students***	***Teacher***	***Students***	***Teacher***	***Students***
Open 3	*Open 0*	*Open 0*	*Open 0*	*Open 5*	*Open 0*
Closed 1	*Closed 0*	*Closed 6*	*Closed 0*	*Closed 0*	*Closed 0*

Attention to these first three layers of effective questioning—looking for patterns of classroom interaction, avoiding automatic, extensive use of closed questions; and crafting open but focused questions—will create a foundation for more productive classroom conversation.

PRACTICE

Finding patterns in classroom interactions requires taping a 5-10 minute segment of a Concept Development lesson. It will help to start taping as a part of your standard practice so that everyone becomes accustomed to and comfortable with the presence of the camera.

Record a few minutes of your Concept Development lesson. Set the camera where it will get the best recording of teacher talk. While student talk is important, the primary focus of this analysis is what you (the teacher) say.

Part 1: Discussion Analysis

Chart the pattern of your classroom conversation using the code below.

T = Talk A = Ask M = Manage

Teacher																						
Students																						

Teacher																						
Students																						

Teacher																						
Students																						

Teacher																						
Students																						

Count the number of times you enter each code for you (Teacher) and for your students. Include a subscript to distinguish between individual students, if desired. Put the totals in the blanks below.

Teacher	***Students***
Talk ______	Talk ______
Ask _______	Ask _______
Open ____	
Closed ____	
Manage _____	Manage_______
	Number Participating_______

Question Count	
Teacher	***Students***
Open ____	*Open* ____
Closed ____	*Closed* ____

Part 2: Reflection

1. List two patterns in your Discussion Analysis that you would like to change, and briefly describe how you might change each:

   a. ____

   ____

   b. ____

   ____

2. What are some ways you could encourage student-to-student conversation during whole-group discussion?

   ____

   ____

   ____

3. What could the teachers in Classrooms A, B, and C have done to encourage students to ask questions?

   ____

   ____

   ____

4. Go back and listen to your recording again. Put a circle around every A that represents an open-ended question and an X over every A that represents a closed question. Count the number of each.

   Open: __________ Closed: __________

Select a closed question, write down the original question, and then rephrase the question so it is open. If there were no closed questions, select an open question and improve its focus:

Original Question: ____

Rephrased Question: ____

References

Ausubel, D. (1963). *The psychology of meaningful verbal learning*. New York: Grune & Stratton.

Durkin, M. C. (1993). *Thinking through class discussion: The Hilda Taba approach.* Lancaster, PA: Technomic.

Institute for Staff Development. (1971). *Hilda Taba teaching strategies program.* Miami, FL: Author.

Maker, C. J. (1982). Hilda Taba teaching strategies program. In C.J. Maker & S.W. Shiever (Eds.), *Teaching Models in education of the gifted* (pp. 237-292). Aspen CO: Aspen Press.

Parsons, T. W. (1969). *Guided self-analysis: A system for professional development.* Berkley, CA: Unversity of California Education Series.

Piaget, J. (1936). *Origins of intelligence in the child.* London: Routledge & Kegan Paul.

Taba, H. (1962). *Curriculum development: Theory and practice.* New York: John Wiley.

Taba, H. (1966). *Teaching strategies and cognitive functioning in elementary school children.* San Francisco: San Francisco State College. (Cooperative Research Project, no. 2404).

Taba, H. (1967). *A teacher's handbook to elementary social studies*. Palo Alto, CA: Addison-Wesley.

Taba, H., Durkin, M. C., Fraenkel, J. R., & McNaughton, A. H. (1971). *A teacher's handbook to elementary social studies: An inductive approach* (2nd ed). Reading, MA: Addison-Wesley.

Taba, H., Levine, S., to & Elzey, F. F. (1967). *Thinking in elementary school children.* San Francisco: San Francisco State College. (Cooperative Research Project, no. 1574).

Tyler, R. W. (1949). *Basic principles of curriculum and instruction*. Chicago: The University of Chicago Press.

Vygotsky, L. S. (1962). *Thought and language.* (E. Hanfmann & G. Vakar, Eds. & Trans.). Cambridge, MA: The M.I.T. Press.

APPENDIX A

THINKING THROUGHOUT CONCEPT DEVELOPMENT

Step 1: List — *Creating a List of Relevant Facts*

What Happens: *Students create a list of about 25 people, places, and/or things related to the lesson.*
Skills Developed: *Recalling information, discriminating between relevant and irrelevant information*
Why Listing Is Important: *As students volunteer items for the list, they reveal their prior knowledge, whether it is information they have just learned in class or information they bring to school from the outside world. As students continue to build the list, they acquire ownership of the knowledge set they will use throughout the lesson. At the same time, their teacher can rest assured that the list will lead to desired learning objectives.*

A Concept Development lesson starts with a list created by the entire class. Even though listing involves the very basic skills of recall and recognition, Taba cautions that it is sometimes worthwhile to spend time:

> *...remembering, savoring, and trying to think of more and more items. The teacher's role is to encourage students to remember as many different things as possible and sometimes even to suggest an item he remembers as a means of getting them out of a mental rut, or a conspiracy of silence.* (Taba et al., 1971)

Of course, lessons gain value when they begin with quality content. Grouping, labeling, and regrouping different kinds of candy will help students become critical thinkers, but grouping, labeling, and regrouping a list of 25 presidents will both develop their thinking skills and help them gain insight into politics, leadership, and historical trends; grouping and regrouping 25 kinds of fruit will reveal similarity and variety in nature.

Asking a focusing question that sets the direction for the list, and then following up with questions that ensure that the list is appropriately diverse, creates the foundation for success.

What Happens: *Students group the items based on a shared attribute. After creating the groups, they create one- to three-word labels for the groups.*
Skills Developed: *Analysis, identifying unique and shared attributes of objects, flexible thinking, word choice and language precision*
Why Grouping and Labeling Are Important: *Grouping. Creating groups requires identifying an object's many attributes and also how its attributes are similar to or different from the attributes of other objects. Recognizing that objects can belong to many different groups opens the door to flexible thinking, serving as a springboard to creativity, perspective, insight, and invention.* *Labeling. When children cluster objects or facts together based on a shared attribute, they automatically take a step away from concrete thinking and toward abstract thinking because the attribute they use as the basis for clustering objects is inherently more abstract than the objects themselves. Labels reveal the level of thinking students use when they cluster objects into groups (see Appendix B).*

Grouping. In order to recognize how two objects are similar, it is necessary to identify their characteristics, or *attributes.* For instance, peaches have soft green leaves, fuzzy skin, sticky juice, yellow-orange flesh, and a hard pit. All of these descriptors, from leaf to pit, are attributes of a peach. Creating groups requires seeing that several different objects have an attribute in common. Peaches aren't the only fruit with a hard pit; nectarines and plums also have this attribute. Establishing groups based on common attributes creates memory networks in the brain that help students retain what they learn. Once the association is made, the words *hard pit* recall not only peaches, but nectarines and plums as well.

Because any given object has many attributes, there are many ways it can be grouped. Peaches, apricots, and kiwis all share *fuzzy skin* in common, but nectarines and plums don't; they wouldn't fit in a *fuzzy skin* group. Peaches, plums, nectarines, apricots, and kiwis are all *fruit* because they carry their seeds inside. Steak doesn't. In fact, steak doesn't seem related to the other objects at all until the mind stretches to consider a broader attribute. Peaches, plums, nectarines, kiwis, and steak are all *food.*

Labeling. Labels create boundaries that define a group, indicating which objects belong in a group and which do not. Labels can be specific or broad; either can be helpful depending on the circumstances. In the example above, peaches, plums, nectarines, and kiwis all fit under the label *fruit,* but *steak* does not. The four fruit and steak do fit under the label *food.* The label *food* provides a more inclusive umbrella than the label *fruit.* Labels can also indicate the nature of a group. If peaches, plums, nectarines, and kiwis were grouped under the label *picnic items,* a whole world of new group members is possible, including napkins, paper plates, Frisbees, and ant repellent. This label suggests divergent thinking that breaks away from self-evident attributes to more far-flung associations. As students acquire the ability to see that objects have many different attributes, they can even begin to group based on two or more shared criteria: peaches, apricots, and nectarines *have hard pits* and *grow on trees.*

Original, unique—but justifiable—connections are at the heart of creative invention. Finding unusual, legitimate attributes shared by different objects begins this kind of divergent thinking. Before it is ripe, a peach could be placed in the group *objects used for playing catch,* along with a baseball. Identifying abstract attributes also promotes creative grouping based on symbolic meaning, as when a peach is grouped with other descriptive terms used to describe qualities of soft skin or ebullient feelings.

Labels sometimes reveal the labeler's point of view. For instance, the war in the United States that began in 1861 was given several different labels, including the Civil War, the War between the States, and the War of Northern Aggression. Each reveals different attitudes toward the same conflict. In the same vein, the labels *healthy snack* or *sweet food* both apply to peaches, kiwis, and grapes, but they send very different messages. Practice in selecting labels inevitably provides opportunities to discuss how the labels assigned to groups affects how they are viewed.

Whether narrow or broad, predictable or off-beat, follow-up questioning is crucial to truly understand the intent behind a student's choice of label. Specific labels can indicate either precise or limited thinking; broad labels can indicate either abstract or vague thinking. Pursuing the reasoning behind a label is a doorway to understanding everything from individual perspective to developmental level. Types of groups are discussed in more detail in Appendix B.

Step 3: Subsume *Cross-Categorizing and Forming Hierarchies*

What Happens: *Young children try to find an object in one group that can also fit in another group. Older children and adolescents form hierarchies of ideas by identifying which groups could fit under the heading of another group. This process entails identifying which labels are broad and which are narrow or more specific.*
Skills Developed: *Cross-categorization, flexible thinking, hierarchical thinking*
Why Subsuming Is Important: *In order to cross-categorize, students must be able to flexibly switch their focus from one attribute to another. A hierarchy creates tiers of ideas, requiring that students can discriminate between smaller, more concrete ideas and larger, more abstract ideas.*

Cross-Categorizing. When one attribute dominates the mind's eye, it can block a person's ability to see other important relationships. Then thinking gets stuck—like only seeing that a peach has fuzz and overlooking its color, texture, pit, and all of the other attributes that make a peach a peach.

Young children tend to see only one way to group an object because they focus on one attribute at a time. Once the peach is placed in the *fuzzy skin* group, they have trouble switching gears to see that a peach could also belong to the *hard pit* group. Learning how to make the mental shift needed to switch focus from one attribute to another is crucial to flexible thinking. Children need practice in identifying the attributes of an object and then grouping that object in different ways based on different attributes. Through this practice, they come to see that a peach has many attributes and can fit into many different groups, including *hard pit*, *fuzzy skin*, *juicy*, or *tree fruit*.

Subsuming. Children must learn to cross-categorize before they can subsume, or create hierarchies. In a hierarchy, objects are automatically cross-categorized because they belong both to a small, specific group and a larger, more abstract group. A peach is both *fruit* and *food* because fruit *is* food. Stated differently, *fruit* can be *subsumed* under the larger category *food* without losing its identity as *fruit*. All of the groups described in the previous section can be organized into a hierarchy of ideas.

- **Food**
  - <u>Fruit</u>
    - <u>Hard Pit</u>
      - Peaches
      - Nectarines
      - Apricots
      - Plums
    - <u>Fuzzy Skin</u>
      - Peaches
      - Kiwis
      - Apricots

Creating hierarchies helps students see which labels are narrow and which are broad, which are concrete and which are abstract. Sometimes it's necessary to go back and revise labels to adjust their breadth in order to make a hierarchy work. Looking at the hierarchy above, it is clear that *steak* and *fruit* don't really belong on the same level. *Steak* could be placed under a label that is parallel to *fruit*, such as *meat*. The process of considering which labels are broad and which are narrow helps students understand the value of different levels of abstraction. More pragmatically, hierarchies are essential elements to organizing essays, projects, and reports.

Step 4: Regroup — Reshaping Perspectives

What Happens: *The groups and labels created in Step 2 are set aside and placed off limits. Students are required to create entirely new groups and labels with the original list created in Step 1.*
Skills Developed: *Analysis, synthesis, divergent thinking, forced analogies, abstract thinking*
Why Regrouping Is Important: *Subsuming requires flexible thinking about an item or a group; regrouping requires that this flexible thinking be applied to the entire list. Students must restructure their mental model of the list, setting aside all of the previous groups and finding new, and often more creative, connections.*

It may seem redundant and perhaps even a waste of time to have children repeat a task they just completed. However, regrouping is actually very different from grouping and labeling. All possibilities are open to students during grouping and labeling, including some that are fairly obvious. Often it is necessary to get these "easy" options out of the way in order to make students search for more original or abstract ideas. This is similar to a process called "forced analogies" used to develop creative thinking skills, in which the task is to find similarities between objects that seem completely different.

Peaches, apricots, kiwis, nectarines, and plums could be grouped any number of ways, but if *hard pit, fuzzy skin,* and *tree fruit* are suddenly off limits, the mind has to stretch to find new ways to cluster them. With coaching and practice, children will learn to search for other associations, finding that these fruit could be separated into groups based on *harvest season, pie fruit, growing region, texture,* or even *nutritional value.*

Step 5: Generalize — Developing Abstract Ideas

What Happens: *Students create general, abstract statements based on the list, groups, labels, and hierarchies created earlier in the lesson.*
Skills Developed: *Synthesis, abstraction*
Why Generalizing Is Important: *Generalizations are unifying ideas that undergird and unite many fields of study. Generalizations help students gain a more sophisticated, complex understanding of information and the rules that govern both nature and human behavior.*

Having worked with the objects on the list in many ways, it is possible to make some general conclusions about the nature of fruit. Sample statements might be: "Fruits look different, but seeds make them alike," or "Most fruits protect their seeds," or even "Most plants around the world share common features." Any of these statements could become the basis for a unit of study about food, botany, or even geography.

APPENDIX B

TYPES OF GROUPS

People are creatures of habit. Habits can help make common life tasks more efficient, but if they take hold too firmly, habits become ruts and harden into closed, dimensionless thinking. One of the benefits of using Concept Development is the access teachers have to hearing whether and how students fall into habitual modes of grouping. This section will describe different ways people create groups and how to encourage students to stay flexible.

Different Ways of Grouping

In many ways, the Concept Development strategy is about the relationship between individual items and groups. Appendix A went into detail about how the varied attributes of an object allow it to be placed in many different kinds of groups. It is equally true that any set of objects can be clustered together into a group for many different reasons. Continuing from the example presented in Appendix A, peaches, plums, and nectarines could be clustered together and labeled *hard pits*, or *picnic food*, or *sustenance*. All three labels are legitimate, yet each describes the items differently. The groups people form usually fall into one of three categories: relational contextual, descriptive, or categorical-inferential.

Relational-Contextual. Relational–contextual groups are formed based on similarities in time, place, or function. In general, this kind of grouping typifies the concrete, experience-based thinking of a very young mind. Teachers of elementary school students, especially in the primary grades, may find that their students frequently group based either on physical attributes or on highly individualized experience. There are three forms of relational-contextual groups:

Locational: Items are found together in the same place.

a. Towel, shower, soap, and faucet go together because they are all found in the bedroom.

b. Florida, Georgia, and Alabama go together because they are in the Southern U.S.

c. Books, magazines, and newspapers go together because they are all found in libraries.

Temporal: Items are grouped because they are related by time.

a. Orange juice, cereal, and toast go together because they are morning food.

b. Sunset and moonrise are grouped because they happen at around the same time.
c. Shoe, whistle, and basketball go together because they are all found on a basketball court during a game.

Functional: Objects are placed in a group because they work together, are used together, or share a cause-effect relationship.

a. Hammer, nail, and wood are grouped because a hammer drives a nail into wood.

b. Horse and cart are grouped because the horse pulls the cart.

c. Tennis racket, tennis ball, and net because the tennis racket hits the ball over (or into) the net.

d. 6, -5, and 1 are grouped because 6 + (-5) = 1.

Descriptive. Groups in this category have items that share the same physical attributes. Subcategories of this type of group include color, material, shape, and appearance. Descriptive groups are somewhat more abstract than relational-contextual groups.

Color: Groups share the same color.

a. Rain, cloud, and fog are grouped because they are all are white or grey.

b. The American and French national flags go together because they are red, white, and blue.

Material: Groups share the same substance, even if they have different colors.

a. Newspaper, magazine, and book are grouped because they are all made of paper.

b. Venus de Milo and Mount Rushmore go together because they are both made of stone.

c. A cup, a window, and a vase go together because they are all made of glass.

Shape: Grouped objects share a similar form.

a. Peru and Switzerland are grouped because both are mountainous.

b. A Rubik's cube and a box of tissues go together because they are both square.
c. Wheat, oats, and rice go together because they are all upright and thin when they grow.

Appearance: Objects are grouped because they look alike in some way other than their color, material, or shape.

a. 50, 302, and 1013 are grouped because they all have one 0 in them.

b. A dog, cat, and squirrel go together because they all have four legs and a tail.

c. A treasure map and a street map go together because they both have squiggly lines.

Categorical-Inferential. Objects in categorical-inferential groups share abstract attributes that cannot be experienced concretely or with the senses. These groups tend to have the broadest scope. Items can be grouped because they perform a similar function, because they share a particular structure, or because they represent a similar idea. As adults, we make groups based on abstract ideas as a matter of course, so it is sometimes difficult to remember that the ability to form this kind of group requires a transformation of thinking in the developing mind of a child. This level of thinking is often not seen until early adolescence. Below are some examples of categorical-inferential groups:

a. Rain, cloud, and fog are grouped, not because they are white or grey, but because they are *forms of weather.*

b. Bicycle, car, plane, and train go together, not because they all have wheels, but because they are *means of transportation.*

c. Drums, cymbals, and xylophones go together, not because they are usually at the back of an orchestra, but because they are *percussion instruments.*

Identifying Group Type.

It is difficult, if not impossible, to determine the type of group students have formed using only the items in the group. Group type is revealed by 1) the *label* selected to describe the group and, more importantly, by 2) *the reasons justifying the choice of label.*

Label and Group Type. The label students choose for their group provides the first clue to how they are thinking about their groups. Consider the example of peaches, plums, and nectarines. They share a number of similarities and could belong to the same group. But what kind of group is it? Depending on how the students are thinking, the objects could be in groups called *tree fruit, fruit with hard pits,* or *nutrition*. None of these is wrong; each group is legitimate and justifiable. Each also suggests that a different kind of thinking was used to form the group. The table on the next page summarizes the differences in thinking behind these three labels.

	Group 1	*Group 2*	*Group 3*
Objects Grouped	Peaches Plums Nectarines	Peaches Plums Nectarines	Peaches Plums Nectarines
Label	Tree Fruit	Fruit with Hard Pits	Nutrition
Reason	They all grow on trees.	Each has a hard pit in the middle.	They are healthy and have vitamins.
Type of Group	Relational-Contextual	Descriptive	Categorical-Inferential

Reasons and Group Type. Sometimes even the label doesn't reveal the basis for a group. Asking the students to describe the reasoning behind their choice of label is essential. Consider the three possible reasons for grouping peaches, plums, and nectarines under the label *tree fruit:*

Tree Fruit Peaches Plums Nectarines	
Reasons	**Group Type**
Because they all grow on trees	Relational-Contextual
Because they all have stems and leaves from trees	Descriptive
Because they all contribute to the life cycle of a tree	Categorical-Inferential

Implications For Teaching Concept Development.

During a Concept Development lesson, it is important to be alert to the types of groups students form in order to break patterns of habitual thinking and introduce new ways of looking at items. This is easiest when there are several different labels under discussion for a group, and students discuss together why each label fits.

The most important element in this process is not to judge or criticize the groups students form, but rather to recognize their grouping patterns so that you can make conscious, deliberate steps to reveal the benefits of viewing objects and groups from different perspectives at increasingly abstract levels.

APPENDIX C

REVIEWING THE CONCEPT DEVELOPMENT TASK

By DR. MARY C. DURKIN

In this writing, I shall try to pull together the kinds of things to keep in mind when thinking about the task of Concept Development.

First of all, I think one should consider the purpose of the task. Teachers use it to assess students' levels of concept development or to encourage them to seek out new relationships as they organize a mass of information. This is the basic function of the task. It does take on a different kind of function at various places in the curriculum as it becomes part of one's teaching style. For example, when one says to a youngster, "Do we really need to handle all of these things separately?" or, "What shall we do about this long list of items?" one is asking concept development questions, not to assess the level of concept development, but rather to organize data. The strategies used here become a part of other cognitive tasks. But essentially, the formal task of concept development consists of listing, grouping, labeling, and subsuming.

Opening the Discussion

The basis for such a discussion with students must have a focus. On the one hand, the opening question should be kept open; on the other hand, it should have focus—not "What will we talk about today?" but, for example, "What did you notice about the new home we saw being built yesterday?" or "What do you know about the people who came to America prior to the Civil War?" So the teacher must set a focus which is related to the purposes of the discussion and, in broader terms, the objectives she seeks to attain.

Opening questions are extremely important. Until teachers begin recording and listening to themselves, they tend to forget about the nature of good opening questions. And although one has brought it up with study groups and talked about asking open-ended questions that many students can respond to, some teachers will still open with a closed question such as, "When did Columbus come to America?" or, "Name three French explorers," so it is important to evaluate opening questions continually. Teachers get into all kinds of difficulties because of their opening question. Sometimes it is too narrow, or it is the kind of question that draws one response—and then a teacher wonders why he cannot get a list up on the chalkboard. He continues by asking another closed question, and again he gets one response; he asks another closed question and gets another single response, and so on. If a teacher is having trouble with the Concept Development task, the first thing he should analyze is the opening question. Is it the type of question that will get out the needed data and get as many students as possible to respond early in the discussion?

It is a good idea to call on the slower students first. They may remember one thing from a film or a reading. This may be the only level at which they are able to contribute, and by calling on the brightest students in the class, one may be doing an injustice to those who have only one thing to contribute. Furthermore, if they do not get a chance to contribute it then, they usually will try to keep it in mind during the whole discussion and mention it at an inappropriate time. If called upon too early, the bright students may dominate the discussion, and in any case, they come up with other things later.

Listing

It is important to keep in mind how much time to spend at the first step of the Concept Development task. It is not necessary to fill the blackboard with items—that becomes unmanageable. One wants to stay at this first step long enough to get the variety of items necessary to carry out one's purposes. Suppose that a teacher asks a group of students the question, "What are some ways in which we use our environment?" As the question is wide open, the students might presume that the teacher wants a variety of items—not just one type of use. If, in response to this question, the students offer swimming, fishing, skating, and skiing, the teacher will have to ask the kind of question that will help them recall other kinds of items. By asking additional questions, the teacher gets out a variety of data that will allow the students to group in such a way that there are sharp distinctions between groups.

Thus, the teacher must be constantly aware of what he wants from the opening question and whether or not the students are giving it to him, and he must move in with other questions if he is not getting it. When does he stop? Either when students start repeating themselves and he feels that they have given him all that they are able to or when at least the slow students have had an opportunity to contribute. Listing goes very quickly if the students have had a common experience.

One matter to consider at this step of concept development is how chains get built in listing and grouping. A teacher has to keep his antenna up all the time, watching for chains and thinking about what to do about them. He has to try to find out what is going on inside the students' minds, supporting those who need support and at the same time seeing that certain material gets listed. The breaking of chains is one of the kinds of things a teacher must think about and do on his feet. An overall question sequence strategy can be developed beforehand, but one can never give the teacher the questions that he needs as he reads his feedback.

Remember, too, that when the students are listing, they are performing the first step of the Concept Development task. They are operating on pure memory. Sometimes students make lists, and then the lists are never used. Now, if a teacher goes to all the trouble of making a list, he should try to use it for several purposes. He may use it later for the correction of errors. Or the list may be added to as new data is gathered. Perhaps it may be used for the task of interpretation of data. Using butcher paper rather than a chalkboard can facilitate multiple uses of a listing.

Before performing this task, teachers should ask themselves the question: What is the most productive way for me to work? Some will want to work with the class as a whole as they go through the steps of listing, grouping, and labeling. However, a more productive way of working is to break the class into pairs or small groups. Many teachers feel that they get a higher level of productivity from students when they use this method. In general, working with others stimulates students. However, a teacher may want to have the students do some parts of the task individually. This also adds variety. Consequently, this kind of activity can be done with almost any size of group.

The important thing is to get data in front of the children in some form. In primary classes, teachers usually have the children draw pictures. Their pictures become the list and are placed along the chalk ledge. All kinds of things can be done with the pictures in the grouping step. Going up to the chalkboard and grouping the pictures allows young children to get up and physically move about. Many young children, as well as certain older children who still need the physical activity, need to do this. At the later levels, students can work from written lists.

Grouping

The second step of the Concept Development task is that of grouping. This is the step in which students start sorting out relationships as they see them. The kind of question that is usually asked at this step is, "Which of these things do you think could go together?" Here, one must be constantly aware of the age of the students one is dealing with. What one usually gets from six- and seven-year-olds is quite different from what one usually gets from teenagers. Also, what students do at these next steps early in the year is much more limited than after several months or years of practice. So one should not set one's expectations too high too early. Piaget has been telling us for 35 years that students will become more effective abstract thinkers if they go through many concrete experiences with those things that are close at hand. That is, if students learn to manipulate concrete things, familiar objects or events—the kind of things that really conjure up images in their minds because they have had concrete experiences with them—they will become better abstract thinkers than if they move to the abstract before they are ready for it. If they skip the concrete operations step and are given labels that have little meaning to them, then they have neither the opportunity nor the power to discover the more abstract relationships.

Follow through. Give students an opportunity to show how they are thinking, and it will be a richer experience for everyone.

Remember that it is important to ask *why*. One can never be certain why students have grouped things together unless they reveal their thinking. This can be done as the students form each group or after all of the groups have been formed.

Dr. Karplus at the University of California at Berkeley tells a story about some seven-year-olds who were grouping and labeling some rocks on their desks. Dr. Karplus was interested in how the students were doing, and so as he walked around the room, he asked one little boy, "How are you grouping your rocks?" and the reply was, "By age."

This was really impressive. So Dr. Karplus said, "Tell me some more about that."

And the little boy replied, "You know, big rocks and little rocks."

It was so easy to be impressed. We give things our own interpretation, as adults. So it is important to ask why to be sure one gets each individual's interpretation.

In a recent test, students were asked to choose the least common denominator for 1/3, 1/4, and 1/6. The figures 6, 12, and 24 were given as choices. One student chose 6, one chose 12, and a third chose 24.

When asked "Why," the student who chose 6 said, "It's the only number that's in the problem."

The student who chose 24 said, "Well, six 4s are 24."

The lucky one who chose 12 said, "Well, 6 and 4 are 10, and 10 and 3 are 13. That's close to 12."

It is important to find many different ways of asking the question *why* because it can be a very threatening kind of word. When I was a classroom teacher, it seemed that when I was exasperated many times by a youngster in trouble, I would ask him, "Why did you do it?" This is the kind of question he gets when he is in trouble, and he gives a sort of frozen response with hunched shoulders. It can block some students. So it might be better to say, for example, "Tell me some more about...," or "How did you happen to put this together?" There are many ways of getting students to reveal their thinking other than asking *why*. Some can take it; others freeze.

Labeling and Subsuming

The next step in the Concept Development task is labeling. This is the step at which students try to reveal what is going on in their head in terms of establishing a hierarchy. They are trying to say that all of these items seem to fit under something that is a little bigger than any one of the items in it. They may not be able to express it very well when they are operating in this manner without saying it explicitly.

I can remember a student who did express this level of thinking quite explicitly one time. The class had made a list in response to the question, "What do you know about California?" and they had a variety of things in their list. Many of them had to do with trees, poppies, bushes, and plants, which they formed into a group. As they looked at this group, one of the students said, "If I was going to put a name on that, I would take out plants and put it on top because they are all plants." He was able to subsume and establish a hierarchy very clearly.

Another group was doing some classification of differences. The teacher asked, "What do you think are some of the differences—not what do you know about Latin America, but what are some of the differences between here and there that you would expect to find if you went to live there?" The class made a long list and grouped the items. They had one group called *products*—silver products, etc. One student said, "I think you would put food under products," and the class seemed to accept this.

All but one boy. He said, "I don't think food would go under products because the question was: How is Latin America different? The people are not different in that they have food. Every country has some kind of food. That's not how they are different. I think that if the person who put it up there was thinking about the way they prepared their food, we would put it under *customs*, and I think that if he meant that it wasn't good food, if it wasn't healthful food, we would put it under *standard of living*." Here was the kind of youngster who is aware of the relationship between the opening question a teacher asks in order to get out data and the ways in which the data should be grouped. He was also aware of the point of view of the person who contributed an item. What the person meant affected the placement of an item. This is the idea of flexibility—point of view. Occasionally, students will become a little uneasy when the grouping does not relate in some way to the reason they gathered the data.

Flexibilty

During a Concept Development task, one needs to be consistently concerned with flexibility. Dr. Karplus, a physicist at the University of California, remarked that too many science teachers emphasize classical categories, such as mammals and reptiles. Students are unable to free themselves to think of relationships in a more creative way. A mammal is a mammal, and that is the end of it. Students give evidence of flexibility when they put an item in more than one group and see that moving an item to another group does not mean that one has to erase it from the first group. Some students have the idea that if an item goes in one group, it cannot possibly go in another group, too. A teacher should encourage his students to accept variety in grouping so that they understand that some of them see things one way and some another, and either way is acceptable. One way of encouraging this idea is to erase all of the groups and labels the students have developed and ask them to form entirely different groups from the list of items.

Other Roles

There are several other teacher roles in Concept Development, and an important one is clarification, which is especially useful when a student gives a label in the listing process. For example, a student might say, "Latin America's exports would be different." When a student comes up with such a group item in the listing step, the teacher should get out the "for instances" so that he can clue other students in as to what was meant and also invite the other students to give additional examples that could fit under the group. We refer to this as extending the discussion. It extends both the participation and the content. At the grouping step, the teacher can invite students who cannot initiate a group to add items to a group or to give additional reasons for the same kind of grouping.

Supporting students whose offerings have been rejected is an important teacher role, as are the roles of focusing and refocusing. Here, one should be careful that, in asking students to group and label, one does not give them a model. If a teacher asks, "Which ones do you think belong together?" it allows the students the opportunity to seek their own relationships and not those suggested by the teacher.

Before starting to group items, it is a good idea to review the list on the board. Youngsters sitting in the back may not be able to read the list very well or remember all of the items. A quick, snappy kind of review (you might have the students read the list) helps them gain momentum to move into grouping.

Whenever possible, try to arrange the students so that they can see and hear each other, for this kind of arrangement encourages pupil-to-pupil discussion. If chairs or desks are movable, a U-shaped arrangement is very effective.

Functions

When does the Concept Development task become functional? Can it be performed in other ways? The answer is yes. When students are arranging bulletin boards or displays, the Concept Development task can help them organize the information they have, but it should reflect the relationships they see. One should resist the temptation to hand students labels or captions and have them put pictures under them. Instead, one should find out how the students see things, what things they would put together, how they would bring order to the mass of information that they have.

When making charts, the Concept Development task becomes really functional as students bring order to a mass of data. They think, "Let's organize things in this way 'cause this is the way I see them, and we will give them this kind of label," and so on. Students in the intermediate and secondary grades should be doing a great deal of this. Any time they make a notebook, they are organizing information. Again, it is best to have the organization develop as they establish the relationships. Too many teachers hand out lists of predetermined relationships or categories for students' notebooks, thus depriving them of the opportunity to go through the process of forming relationships.

Readiness

Whatever grade level you teach, expect a wide range in the kinds of results you get from students. Certainly with young children, a teacher can expect there to be a functional or egocentric kind of grouping—for example, "I'd put bananas with corn flakes because I like bananas and corn flakes together." It does not occur to this child that someone else may put berries on his corn flakes. He thinks, "I do it this way. This is the way I would group it." However, leave things open for the child who does have a different kind of perspective and who can see things more objectively. In other words, impose no ceilings on children—leave the process open.

Seven- to 12-year olds tend to group mainly on a functional or descriptive basis. But many children of that age will go to the more abstract class-type basis, and 12- to 15-year-olds should begin to use highly abstract kinds of grouping. Always remember that there is a continuum, that even at older ages, children may put things together on a functional basis. There is overlapping at every age. Furthermore, a student's grouping behavior is apt to differ according to the kinds of data he is working with; if he is using data with which he is very familiar, he is more apt to be abstract than if he is confronted with data that is strange to him.

The important thing is to provide opportunities for students of any age to establish relationships among the mass of data to which they are exposed in their world. It is in this way that they learn to order things in their life and become able to confront problems more effectively.

APPENDIX D

BLANK FORMS

LESSON PLAN: CONCEPT DEVELOPMENT

Purpose of Discussion: ______________________________

Grade Level: ______________________________

Background Information for Lesson: ______________________________

Concept Development	*Focusing Questions*	*Materials and Supports*
Step 1: List		
Step 2: Group and Label	Grouping: Labeling:	
Step 3: Subsume		
Step 4: Regroup		
Step 5: Generalize		

Cognitive Map for Concept Development

Purpose of Discussion: ____

Possible List (Step 1)	Possible Groups and Labels (Step 2)	Possible Subsuming (Step 3)
		Possible Regroups and Labels (Step 4)
Possible Generalizations (Step 5): Five is made of many combinations. The order of the numbers does not matter when adding.		

Cognitive Map format adapted from: Institute for Staff Development (1971).

Classroom Interaction Analysis

Record five minutes of your Concept Development lesson. Use the chart below, and chart the path of your classroom conversation using the code:

T = Talk A = Ask M = Manage

Teacher																						
Students																						

Teacher																						
Students																						

Teacher																						
Students																						

Teacher																						
Students																						

Count the number of times you enter each code for you and for your combined students. Put the totals in the blanks below.

Teacher	***Students***
Teacher Talk ______	Students Talk ______
Teacher Ask ______	Students Ask ______
Teacher Manage______	Students Manage______
	Number of Students Participating ______